MW00986811

SHE ADDED WOOD TO THE FIRE

A Little Maid of Old Maine

BY

Alice Turner Curtis

AUTHOR OF
The "Little Maid" Historical Books,
"Yankee Girls" Civil War Stories

Illustrated by
Elizabeth Pilsbry

Applewood Books
Bedford, Massachusetts

A Little Maid of Old Maine was first published by the Penn Publishing Company in 1920.

ISBN 1-55709-336-9

Thank you for purchasing an Applewood Book.
Applewood reprints America's lively classics—
books from the past that are still of interest to modern readers.
For a free copy of our current catalog, write to:
Applewood Books, P.O. Box 365, Bedford, MA 01730.

10 9 8 7 6 5 4 3 2 1

Printed and bound in Canada.

Library of Congress Cataloging-in-Publication Data
Curtis, Alice Turner.
A little maid of Old Maine / by Alice Turner Curtis; illustrated by Elizabeth Pilsbry.
p. cm.
Summary: To help the men of Machias, Maine, capture an English gunboat in June 1775, Rebecca and Anna undertake a dangerous journey through a forest to get ammunition for them.
ISBN 1-55709-336-9
1. Maine—History—Revolution, 1775–1783—Juvenile fiction. [1. Maine—History—Revolution, 1775–1783 —Fiction. 2. United States—History—Revolution, 1775–1783 —Fiction.] I. Pilsbry, Elizabeth, ill. II. Title

PZ7.C941 Lml 1999
[Fid]—dc21

99-042220

Introduction

"A LITTLE MAID OF OLD MAINE" is a true story of the brave effort of two girls to bring help to a little settlement on the Maine coast at the time of the War of the Revolution. Parson Lyon, the father of Melvina, was a friend and correspondent of Washington, and the capture of the English gunboat by the Machias men is often referred to in history as "The Lexington of the Seas," being the first naval battle after the Lexington encounter.

The story is based on facts, and its readers cannot fail to be interested and touched by the courage and patriotism of Rebecca and Anna Weston as they journeyed through the forest after the powder that was to make possible the conquest of America's foe.

CONTENTS

ILLUSTRATIONS

A Little Maid of Old Maine

CHAPTER I

A LIBERTY POLE

ANNA and Rebecca Weston, carrying a big basket between them, ran along the path that led from their home to the Machias River. It was a pleasant May morning in 1775, and the air was filled with the fragrance of the freshly cut pine logs that had been poled down the river in big rafts to be cut into planks and boards at the big sawmills. The river, unusually full with the spring rains, dashed against its banks as if inviting the little girls to play a game with it. Usually Anna and Rebecca were quite ready to linger at the small coves which crept in so near to the footpath, and sail boats made of pieces of birch-bark, with alder twigs for masts and broad oak leaves for sails. They named these boats *Polly* and *Unity*, after the two fine sloops which carried lumber from Machias to Boston and returned with cargoes of provisions for the little settlement.

But this morning the girls hurried along without a thought for such pleasant games. They were both anxious to get to the lumber yard as soon as possible, not only to fill their basket with chips, as their mother had bidden them, but to hear if there were not some news of the *Polly*, the return of which was anxiously awaited; for provisions were getting scarce in this remote village, and not until the *Polly* should come sailing into harbor could there be any sugar cakes, or even bread made of wheat flour.

As they hurried along they heard the cheerful whistle of Mr. Worden Foster, the blacksmith, who was just then taking a moment of well-earned leisure in the door of his shop, and stood looking out across the quiet waters of the river and harbor. As the girls came near he nodded pleasantly, but did not stop whistling. People in Machias declared that the blacksmith woke up in the morning whistling, and never stopped except to eat. And, indeed, his little daughter Luretta said that when her father wanted a second helping of anything at the table he would whistle and point toward it with his knife; so it might be said that Mr. Foster whistled even at his meals.

"There's Father! There's Father!" Anna called out as they passed a big pile of pine logs and came to where stacks of smooth boards just from the sawmill shut the river from sight.

"Well, Danna, do you and Rebby want your basket filled with golden oranges from sunny Italy and dates from Egypt? Or shall it be with Brazilian nuts and ripe pineapples from South America?"

"Oh, Father! Say some more!" exclaimed Anna, laughing with delight; for she never tired of hearing her father tell of the wonderful fruits of far-off lands that he had seen in his sailor days, before he came to live in the little settlement of Machias, in the Province of Maine, and manage the big sawmill.

"Father, tell us, is the *Polly* coming up the bay?" Rebecca asked eagerly. She had a particular reason for wanting the sloop to reach harbor as soon as possible, for her birthday was close at hand, and her father had told her that the *Polly* was bringing her a fine gift; but what it was Rebecca could not imagine. She had guessed everything from a gold ring to a prayer-book; but at every guess her father had only smilingly shook his head.

"No sign of the *Polly* yet, Rebby," Mr. Weston replied.

Rebecca sighed as her father called her "Rebby," and a little frown showed itself on her forehead. She was nearly fourteen, and she had decided that neither "Rebecca" nor "Rebby" were names that suited her. Her middle name was "Flora," and only that morning Anna had promised not to call her by any other name save Flora in future.

Mr. Weston smiled down at Rebecca's serious face.

"So 'tis not spices from far Arabia, or strings of pink coral, this morning," he continued, taking the basket, "but pine chips. Well, come over here and we will soon fill the basket," and he led the way to where two men were at work with sharp adzes smoothing down a big stick of timber.

In a few minutes the basket was filled, and the little girls were on their way home.

"Would it not be a fine thing, Rebby, if we could really fill our basket with pineapples and sweet-smelling spices?" said Anna, her brown eyes looking off into space, as if she fancied she could see the wonderful things of which her father spoke; "and do you not wish that we were both boys, and could go sailing off to see far lands?"

"Anna! Only this morning you promised to call me 'Flora,' and now it is 'Rebby,' 'Rebby.' And as for 'far lands'—of course I don't want to see them. Have you not heard Father say that there were no more beautiful places in all the world than the shores of this Province?" responded Rebecca reprovingly. She sometimes thought that it would have been far better if Anna had really been a boy instead of a girl; for the younger girl delighted to be called "Dan," and had persuaded her mother to keep her brown curls cut short "like a boy's"; beside this, Anna cared little for dolls, and was completely happy when her father would take her with him for a day's deep-sea fishing, an excursion which Rebecca could never be persuaded to attempt. Anna was also often her father's companion on long tramps in the woods, where he went to mark trees to be cut for timber. She wore moccasins on these trips, made by the friendly Indians who often visited the little settlement, and her mother had made her a short skirt of tanned deer-skin, such as little Indian girls sometimes wear, and with her blue blouse of homespun flannel, and round cap with a partridge wing on one side, Anna looked like a real little daughter of the woods as she trotted sturdily along beside her tall father.

As the sisters passed the blacksmith shop they could hear the ringing stroke on the anvil, for Mr. Foster had returned to his work of hammering out forks for pitching hay and grain; these same forks which were fated to be used before many months passed as weapons against the enemies of American liberty.

"To-morrow I am to go with Father to the woods," announced Anna as they came in sight of the comfortable log cabin which stood high above the river, and where they could see their mother standing in the doorway looking for their return. The girls waved and called to their mother as they hurried up the path.

"We have fine chips, Mother," called Rebecca, while Anna in a sing-song tone called out: "Pineapples and sweet-smelling spices! Strings of pink coral and shells from far lands."

Rebecca sighed to herself as she heard Anna's laughing recital of their father's words. She resolved to ask her mother to forbid Anna talking in future in such a silly way.

"You are good children to go and return so promptly," said Mrs. Weston, "but you are none too soon, for 'twill take a good blow with the bellows to liven up the coals, and I have a fine venison steak to broil for dinner," and as she spoke Mrs. Weston took the basket and hurried into the house, followed by the girls.

"Mother, what is a 'liberty pole'?" questioned Anna, kneeling on the hearth to help her mother start the fire with the pine chips.

"What dost thou mean, child? Surely the men are not talking of such matters as liberty poles?" responded her mother anxiously.

Anna nodded her head. "Yes, Mother. There is to be a 'liberty pole' set up so it can be well seen from the harbor, for so I heard Mr. O'Brien say; and Father is to go to the woods to-morrow to find it. It is to be the straightest and handsomest sapling pine to be found in a day's journey; that much I know," declared Anna eagerly; "but tell me why is it to be called a 'liberty pole'? And why is it to be set up so it can be well seen from the harbor?"

"Thou knowest, Anna, that King George of England is no longer the true friend of American liberty," said Mrs Weston, "and the liberty pole is set up to show all Tories on land or sea that we mean to defend our homes. And if the men are talking of putting up the tree of liberty in Machias I fear that trouble is near at hand. But be that as it may, our talking of such matters will not make ready thy father's dinner. Blaze up the fire with these chips, Anna; and thou, Rebby, spread the table."

Both the girls hastened to obey; but Anna's thoughts were pleasantly occupied with the morrow's excursion when she would set forth with her father to discover the "handsome sapling pine tree," which was to be erected as the emblem of the loyalty of the Machias settlement to Freedom's call. Anna knew they would follow one of the Indian trails through the forest, where she would see many a wild bird, and that the day would be filled with delight.

But Rebecca's thoughts were not so pleasant. Here it was the fifth of May, and no sign of the *Polly*, and on the tenth she would be fourteen; and not a birthday gift could she hope for unless the sloop arrived. Beside this, the talk of a liberty pole in Machias made her anxious and unhappy. Only yesterday she had spent the afternoon with her most particular friend, Lucia Horton, whose father was captain of the *Polly*; and Lucia had told Rebecca something of such importance, after vowing her to secrecy, that this talk of a liberty pole really frightened her. And the thought that her own father was to select it brought the danger very near. She wished that Lucia had kept the secret to herself, and became worried and unhappy.

Rebecca was thinking of these things, and not of spreading the table, when she went to the cupboard to bring out the pewter plates, and she quite forgot her errand until her mother called:

"Rebby! Rebby! What are you about in the cupboard?" Then, bringing only one plate instead of four, she came slowly back to the kitchen.

"What ails the child?" questioned Mrs. Weston sharply. "I declare, I believe both of my children are losing their wits. Here is Anna making rhymes and sing-songing her words in strange fashion; and thou, Rebecca a girl of nearly fourteen, careless of thy work, and standing before me on one foot like a heron, staring at naught," and Mrs. Weston hurried to the pantry for the forgotten dishes.

Anna smiled at her mother's sharp words, for she did not mind being called a silly girl for rhyming words. " 'Tis no harm," thought Anna, "and my father says 'tis as natural as for the birds to sing"; so she added more chips to the fire, and thought no more of it.

But Rebecca, who was used to being praised for her good sense and who was seldom found fault with, had looked at her mother in surprise, and the pewter plate fell from her hands and went clattering to the floor. At that moment the door swung open and Mr. Weston entered the kitchen.

"Father! Father!" exclaimed Rebecca, running toward him, "you won't put up a liberty pole, will you? You won't! Promise you won't, Father!" and she clasped his arm with both hands.

CHAPTER II

REBECCA'S SECRET

Mr. Weston looked down smilingly at his little daughter. He was evidently amused at her excitement.

"Is this the little girl who was born in loyal Boston?" he questioned; for Rebecca was six years of age and Anna three when their parents came to this far-off place to make their home. Eastern Maine was then a wilderness, and this little village was not connected with the outside world except by the Indian trails or by the sailing craft which plied up and down the coast. But its citizens were soon to write a page of heroism and valor in their country's history.

"Of course Machias is to have a liberty pole,"continued Mr. Weston. "It has been so decided by a vote in a town meeting; and Dan and I will start off in good season to-morrow morning to look for the finest pine sapling in the forest. It will be a great day for the village when 'tis set up, with its waving green plume to show that we are pledged to resist England's injustice to her long-suffering colonies."

It was the custom to leave a tuft of verdure at the top of the liberty tree as an emblem, the best they had at command, of the flag they meant to fight for.

Before her father had finished speaking Rebecca had relinquished her grasp on his arm and ran toward the cupboard, and neither her father nor mother gave much thought to her anxious question. The venison was just ready to serve, and Mrs. Weston hurried from the fireplace to the table, on which Rebecca had now placed the dishes, while Mr. Weston and Anna talked happily together over the proposed excursion on the following day.

"I am afraid that we may have to postpone our journey," said Mr. Weston, "for I noticed the gulls were coming in flocks close to the shore, and you know:

" 'When sea-birds fly to land
A storm is at hand.' "

"But look at Malty," responded Anna quickly, pointing to the fat Maltese cat who was industriously washing her face:

" 'If the cat washes her face over the ear
'Tis a sign the weather'll be fine and clear,' "

quoted the little girl; "and you told me 'twas a sure sign, Father; and 'tis what Malty is doing this minute."

"To be sure," laughed Mr. Weston, "both are sure signs, and so we will hope for fair weather."

Rebecca was very silent at dinner, and as the sisters began to clear away the dishes Anna watched her with troubled eyes.

"Perhaps it's because I called her 'Rebby,'" thought the little girl regretfully. "I'll tell her I am sorry," and when their mother left the kitchen Anna whispered:

"Flora, I forgot when I called you 'Rebby.' But I will now surely remember. You are not vexed at me, are you?" and Anna leaned her head against her sister's arm and looked up at her pleadingly.

Rebecca sniffed a little, as if trying to keep back the tears. She wished she could talk over her worries with Anna; but of course that would never do.

"I believe I'd rather be called 'Rebby,'" she managed to say, to the surprise of her younger sister. "Do you suppose they really mean to put up a liberty pole?"

"Of course," responded Anna. "I heard the minister say that it must be done."

Rebby sighed dolefully. She was old enough to understand the talk she heard constantly of His Majesty's ships of war capturing the American fishing sloops, and of the many troubles caused to peaceable Americans all along the coast; and she, like all the American children, knew that their rights must be defended; but Lucia Horton's talk had frightened and confused Rebecca's thoughts. To set up a liberty pole now seemed to her a most dangerous thing to do, and something that would bring only trouble.

She wished with all her heart that she could tell her father all that Lucia had told her. But that she could not do because of her promise. Rebecca knew that a promise was a sacred thing, not to be broken.

"Rebby, will you not go to the bluff with me? 'Twill be pleasant there this afternoon, and we could see the *Polly* if she chances to come into harbor to-day," said Anna.

"You had best ask Luretta Foster, Danna," she answered quickly. "I am sure Mother will want my help with her quilting this afternoon."

Rebby so often played at being "grown up" that this reply did not surprise Anna, and she ran off to find her mother and ask permission to go to the shore with Luretta Foster, a girl of about her own age. Mrs. Weston gave her consent, and in a few moments the little girl was running along the river path toward the blacksmith shop where a short path led to Luretta's home.

Anna often thought that there could not be another little girl in all the world as pretty as Luretta. Luretta was not as tall or as strongly made as Anna; her eyes were as blue as the smooth waters of the harbor on a summer's day; her hair was as yellow as the floss on an ear of corn, and her skin was not tanned brown like Anna's, but was fair and delicate. Beside her Anna looked more like a boy than ever. But Luretta admired Anna's brown eyes and short curly hair, and was quite sure that there was no other little girl who could do or say such clever things as Anna Weston. So the two little girls were always well pleased with each other's company, and to-day Luretta was quite ready to go down to the shore and watch for the *Polly*. Mrs. Foster tied on the big sunbonnet which Luretta always wore out-of-doors, and the two friends started off.

"Will it not be fine if the *Polly* reaches harbor to-day?" said Anna. "My father says she will bring sugar and molasses and spices, and it may be the *Unity* will come sailing in beside her loaded with things from far lands. Do you not wish our fathers were captains of fine sloops, Luretta, so that perhaps we could go sailing off to Boston?"

But Luretta shook her head. "I'd much rather journey by land," she answered; "but 'tis said the *Polly* is to bring a fine silk gown for Mistress Lyon; 'tis a present from her sister in Boston, and two dolls for Melvina Lyon. Why is it that ministers' daughters have so many gifts?" and Luretta sighed. Her only doll was made of wood, and, though it was very dear to her, Luretta longed for a doll with a china head and hands, such as the fortunate little daughter of the minister already possessed.

"I care not for Melvina Lyon, if she be a minister's daughter," Anna responded bravely. "She can do nothing but sew and knit and make fine cakes, and read from grown-up books. She is never allowed to go fishing, or wade in the cove on warm days, or go off in the woods as I do. I doubt if Melvina Lyon could tell the difference 'twixt a partridge and heron, or if she could tell a spruce tree from a fir. And as for presents, hers are of no account. They are but dolls, and silver thimbles and silk aprons. Why! did not my father bring me home a fine beaver skin for a hood, and a pair of duck's wings, and a pair of moccasins the very last time he went north!" And Anna, out of breath, looked at her friend triumphantly.

"But Melvina's things are all bought in stores in big towns, and your presents are all from the woods, just as if you were a little Indian girl," objected Luretta, who greatly admired the ruffled gowns of Melvina's dolls, such as no other little girl in the settlement possessed.

Anna made no response to this; but she was surprised that Luretta should not think as she did about the value of her gifts, and rather vexed that Melvina Lyon should be praised by her own particular friend.

The girls had passed the sawmill and lumber yard, and now turned from the well-traveled path to climb a hill where they could catch the first glimpse of any sail entering the harbor. Farther along this bluff stood the church, not yet quite finished, and beyond it the house of the minister, the Reverend James Lyon, whose little daughter, Melvina, was said to be the best behaved and the smartest girl in the settlement. Although only ten years old Melvina had already "pieced" four patchwork quilts and quilted them; and her neat stitches were the admiration of all the women of the town. But most of the little girls were a little in awe of Melvina, who never cared to play games, and always brought her knitting or sewing when she came for an afternoon visit.

Anna and Luretta sat down on the short grass, and for a few moments talked of the *Polly*, and looked in vain for the glimmer of a sail.

"Look, Danna! Here comes Melvina now," whispered Luretta, whose quick ears had caught the sound of steps.

Anna looked quickly around. "She's all dressed up," she responded. "See, her skirts set out all around her like a wheel."

Melvina walked with great care, avoiding the rough places, and so intent on her steps that, if Anna had not called her name, she would have passed without seeing them. She was thin and dark, and looked more like a little old lady than a ten-year-old girl.

"How do you do?" she said, bowing as ceremoniously as if Luretta and Anna were grown-up people of importance.

"Come and sit down, Melly, and watch for the *Polly*," said Anna.

"And tell us about the fine dolls that are on board for you," added Luretta quickly.

A little smile crept over Melvina's face and she took a step toward them, but stopped suddenly.

"I fear 'twould not be wise for me to stop," she said a little fearfully; but before she could say anything more Anna and Luretta had jumped up and ran toward her.

"Look!" exclaimed Anna, pointing to a flock of white gulls that had just settled on the smooth water near the shore.

"Look, Melly, at the fine partridges!"

Melvina's dark eyes looked in the direction Anna pointed. "Thank you, Anna. How white they are, and what a queer noise they make," she responded seriously.

Anna's eyes danced with delight as she heard Luretta's half-repressed giggle at Melvina's reply. She resolved that Luretta should realize of how little importance Melvina Lyon, with all her dolls, and her starched skirts like wheels, really was.

"And are those not big alder trees, Melly?" she continued, pointing to a group of fine pine trees near by.

Again Melvina's eyes followed the direction of Anna's pointing finger, and again the minister's little daughter replied politely that the trees were indeed very fine alders.

Luretta was now laughing without any effort to conceal her amusement. That any little girl in Maine should not know a partridge from a gull, or an alder bush from a pine tree, seemed too funny to even make it necessary to try to be polite; and Luretta was now ready to join in the game of finding out how little Melvina Lyon, "the smartest and best-behaved child in the settlement," really knew.

"And, Danna, perhaps Melvina has never seen the birds we call clams?" she suggested.

Melvina looked from Anna to Luretta questioningly. These little girls could not be laughing at her, she thought, recalling with satisfaction that it was well known that she could spell the names of every city in Europe, and repeat the list of all England's kings and queens. She remembered, also, that Anna Weston was called a tomboy, and that her mother said it was a scandal for a little girl to have short hair. So she again replied pleasantly that she had never known that clams were birds. "We have them stewed very often," she declared.

Anna fairly danced about the neat little figure in the well-starched blue linen skirt.

"Oh, Melly! You must come down to the shore, and we will show you a clam's nest," she said, remembering that only yesterday she had discovered the nest of a kingfisher in an oak tree whose branches nearly touched the shore, and could point this out to the ignorant Melvina.

"But I am to visit Lucia Horton this afternoon, and I must not linger," objected Melvina.

"It will not take long," urged Anna, clasping Melvina's arm, while Luretta promptly grasped the other, and half led, half pushed the surprised and uncertain Melvina along the rough slope. Anna talked rapidly as they hurried along. "You ought really to see a clam's nest," she urged, between her bursts of laughter; "why, Melly, even Luretta and I know about clams."

Anna had not intended to be rude or cruel when she first began her game of letting Luretta see that Melly and her possessions were of no importance, but Melvina's ignorance of the common things about her, as well as her neatly braided hair, her white stockings and kid shoes, such as no other child in the village possessed, made Anna feel as if Melvina was not a real little girl, but a dressed-up figure. She chuckled at the thought of Luretta's calling clams "birds," with a new admiration for her friend.

"I guess after this Luretta won't always be talking about Melvina Lyon and her dolls," she thought triumphantly; and at that moment Melvina's foot slipped and all three of the little girls went sliding down the sandy bluff.

The slide did not matter to either Anna or Luretta, in their stout shoes and every-day dresses of coarse flannel, but to the carefully dressed Melvina it was a serious mishap. Her starched skirts were crushed and stained, her white stockings soiled, and her slippers scratched. The hat of fine-braided straw with its ribbon band, another "present" from the Boston relatives, now hung about her neck, and her knitting bag was lost.

As the little girls gathered themselves up Melvina began to cry. Her delicate hands were scratched, and never before in her short life had she been so frightened and surprised.

She pulled herself away from Anna's effort to straighten her hat. "You are a rough child," she sobbed, "and I wish I had not stopped to speak with you. And my knitting bag with my half-finished stocking is lost!"

At the sight of Melvina's tears both Anna and Luretta forgot all about showing her a "clam's nest," and became seriously frightened. After all, Melly was the minister's daughter, and the Reverend Mr. Lyon was a person of importance; why, he even had a colored body-servant, London Atus by name, who usually walked behind the clergyman carrying his cloak and Bible, and who opened the door for visitors. Often Melvina was attended in her walks by London, who thought his little mistress far superior to the other children.

"Don't cry, Melvina," pleaded Luretta. "We will find your bag, and we will wash the stains from your stockings and dress, and help you back up the slope. Don't cry," and Luretta put a protecting arm about the frightened Melvina. "Your hat has only slipped from your head; it is not hurt at all," she added consolingly.

Melvina was finally comforted, and Anna climbed up the slope to search for the missing bag, while Luretta persuaded Melvina to take off her stockings in order that they might be washed.

"They'll dry in no time," Luretta assured her. "I can wash them out right here in this clean puddle, and put them on the warm rocks to dry." So Melvina reluctantly took off her slippers, and the pretty open-work stockings, and curling her feet under her, sat down on a big rock to watch Luretta dip the stockings in the little pool of sea water near by, and to send anxious glances toward the sandy bluff where Anna was searching for the missing bag.

CHAPTER III

MELVINA MAKES DISCOVERIES

THE sun shone warmly down on the brown ledges, the little waves crept up the shore with a pleasant murmur, and Melvina, watching Luretta dipping her white stockings in the pool, began to feel less troubled and unhappy; and when Anna came running toward her waving the knitting-bag she even smiled, and was ready to believe that her troubles were nearly over.

In spite of the sunshine dark clouds were gathering along the western horizon; but the girls did not notice this. Anna and Luretta had forgotten all about the sloop *Polly*, and were both now a little ashamed of their plan to make sport of Melvina.

"Here is your bag all safe, Melly," called Anna, "and while Luretta is washing your stockings I'll rub off those spots on your pretty dress. Can't you step down nearer the water?" she suggested, handing the bag to Melvina, who put it carefully beside her hat and agreed promptly to Anna's suggestion, stepping carefully along the rough shore to the edge of the water. The rocks hurt her tender feet, but she said nothing; and when she was near the water she could not resist dipping first one foot and then the other in the rippling tide.

"Oh, I have always wanted to wade in the ocean," she exclaimed, "and the water is not cold."

As Anna listened to Melvina's exclamation a new and wonderful plan came into her thoughts; something she decided that would make up to Melvina for her mischievous fun. She resolved quickly that Melvina Lyon should have the happiest afternoon of her life.

"Melly, come back a little way and slip off your fine skirts. I'll take off my shoes and stockings and we'll wade out to Flat Rock and back. Luretta will fix your clothes, won't you, Lu?" she called, and Luretta nodded.

The stains did not seem to come out of the stockings; they looked gray and streaked, so Luretta dipped them again, paying little attention to her companions.

Melvina followed Anna's suggestion, and her starched skirts and hat were left well up the beach with Anna's stout shoes and stockings, and the two girls hurried back hand in hand to the water's edge.

Flat Rock was not far out from the shore, and Anna knew that the pebbly beach ended in soft mud that would not hurt Melvina's feet, so she led her boldly out.

"WE'LL WADE OUT TO FLAT ROCK"

"It's fun," declared Melvina, her dark eyes dancing as she smiled at Anna, quite forgetting all her fears.

"It would be more fun if we had on real old clothes and could splash," responded Anna; and almost before she finished speaking Melvina leaned away from her and with her free hand swept the water toward her, spraying Anna and herself. In a moment both the girls had forgotten all about their clothes, and were chasing each other along the water's edge splashing in good earnest, and laughing and calling each other's names in wild delight. Farther up the shore Luretta, a draggled stocking in each hand, looked at them a little enviously, and wondered a little at the sudden change in Melvina's behavior.

"Now show me the clam's nest!" Melvina demanded, as out of breath and thoroughly drenched the two girls stood laughing at each other.

"All right," Anna responded promptly. "Come on down to the point," and followed by Melvina, now apparently careless of the rough beach, she ran along the shore toward a clam bed in the dark mud.

"Look!" she exclaimed, pointing to the black flats-mud. "There is the clam's nest—in that mud. Truly. They are not birds; they are shell-fish. I was only fooling."

"I don't care," answered Melvina. "I shall know now what clams really are."

"And those birds are gulls, not partridges," continued Anna, pointing to the flock of gulls near shore, "and come here and I will show you a real alder," and the two girls climbed over a ledge to where a little thicket of alder bushes crept down close to the rocks.

"And those splendid tall trees are pines," went on Anna, pointing to the group of tall trees on the bluff.

Melvina laughed delightedly. "Why, you know all about everything," she exclaimed, " even if your hair is short like a boy's."

"I know all the trees in the forest," declared Anna, "and I know where squirrels hide their nuts for winter, and where beavers make their houses in the river."

The two girls were now beyond the ledge and out of sight of Luretta, and Anna was so eager to tell Melvina of the wonderful creatures of the forest, and Melvina, feeling as if she had discovered a new world, listened with such pleasure, that for the moment they both forgot all about Luretta.

At first Luretta had been well pleased to see that Melvina was no longer vexed and unhappy; but when both her companions disappeared, and she found herself alone with Melvina's soiled and discarded skirts and the wet stockings, she began to feel that she was not fairly treated, and resolved to go home.

"Dan can play with Melvina Lyon if she likes her so much," thought Luretta resentfully, and started off up the slope. Luretta was nearly as tidy as when she left home, so she would have no explanations to make on her return. As she went up the slope she turned now and then and looked back, but there was no sign of Anna or Melvina. "I don't care," thought the little girl unhappily. "Perhaps they will think I am drowned when they come back and don't find me." She had just reached the top of the slope and turned toward home when she saw London Atus hurrying along the path that led to the church.

"Perhaps he has been sent after Melvina, and can't find her," thought Luretta; and she was right; the colored man had been to Captain Horton's house to walk home with his little mistress, and had been told that Melvina had not been there that afternoon; and he was now hurrying home with this alarming news.

Anna and Melvina were now comfortably seated on a grassy knoll near the alder bushes, Melvina asking questions about woodland birds, and the wild creatures of the forest, which Anna answered with delight.

"Perhaps you can go with Father and me to the forest to-morrow," said Anna. "We are going to find a liberty pole, and 'twill be a fine walk."

"I know about liberty poles," declared Melvina eagerly, " and my father is well pleased that the town is to set one up. But, oh, Anna! surely it is time that I went on to my visit with Lucia Horton!" and Melvina's face grew troubled. "Do you think Luretta Foster will have my clothes in good order?"

At Melvina's words Anna sprang to her feet. "I think she will do her best, and 'tis well for us to hurry," she responded; "but you have had a good time, have you not, Melvina?"

"Oh, yes! I would like well to play about on the shore often; but I fear I may never again," said Melvina; her smile had vanished, and she looked tired and anxious.

"Let us hasten; the tide is coming in now, and Luretta will have taken our things up from the beach," said Anna, taking Melvina's hand and hurrying her along over the ledges. "I am glad indeed, Melvina, that we are better acquainted, and we will often wade together."

But Melvina shook her head dolefully. "My mother does not like me to play out-of-doors," she said. "Do you think, Anna, that Luretta is quite sure to have my things clean and nice?"

The two little girls had now come in sight of the place where they had left Luretta. They both stopped and looked at each other in dismay, for the tide had swept up the beach covering the pool where Luretta had endeavored to wash the stockings, and the rocks where Anna and Melvina had left their things, and there was no trace either of Luretta or of their belongings.

"Luretta has taken our things up the slope," declared Anna. "She saw the tide would sweep them away, so she did not wait for us."

"But how can we find her?" wailed Melvina. "I cannot go up the slope barefooted and in my petticoat. What would my father say if he met me in such a plight? He tells me often to remember to set a good example to other children. And I would be ashamed indeed to be seen like this."

"You do look funny," Anna acknowledged soberly. Her own flannel dress had dried, and, except for her bare feet, she looked about as usual; but Melvina's white petticoat was still wet and draggled, her hair untidy, and it was doubtful if her own father would have recognized her at the first glance.

"I will go and get your things," said Anna. "Come up the slope a little way, and sit down behind those juniper bushes until I come back. Luretta must be near the pine trees. I'll hurry right back, and you can dress in a minute."

Melvina agreed to this plan, and followed Anna slowly up to the juniper bushes, and crouched down well under their branches so that she was completely hidden from view; while Anna scrambled hurriedly up the slope and looked anxiously about for some sign of Luretta and the missing garments. But there was no sign of either; so she ran along the bluff to where the pines offered shelter, thinking Luretta must surely be there.

And now Anna began to be seriously alarmed. Perhaps Luretta had been swept out by the tide before she could save herself. And at this thought Anna forgot all about shoes and stockings, all Melvina's fine garments, and even Melvina herself, and ran as fast as her feet could carry her toward Luretta's home. At the blacksmith shop she stopped to take breath, and to see if Luretta might not, by some happy chance, be there; but the shop was silent. Mr. Foster had gone home to his supper; but Anna did not realize that the hour was so late, and ran swiftly on.

As she neared the house she stopped suddenly, for Luretta was standing in the doorway, and Rebecca was beside her, and they were both looking at Anna. There was no time to turn and run back.

"Why, Dan! Where are your shoes and stockings?" said Rebecca, coming down the path to meet her sister. "You were so late in coming home that Mother sent me to meet you."

"What did Luretta say?" gasped Anna, thinking to herself that if Luretta had told of Melvina, and their making sport of her, that there was trouble in store for them all.

"Luretta hadn't time to say anything," responded Rebecca, "for I had just reached the door when we saw you coming. Now we'll get your shoes and stockings and start home, for Mother is waiting supper for us."

"Luretta has my shoes," said Anna, and ran on to the door, where Luretta was still waiting.

"Give me my shoes and stockings; quick, Lu! And then take all Melvina's things and run, as fast as you can, to the——"

"Luretta! Luretta!" called Mrs. Foster; and Luretta with a hurried whisper: "Oh, Anna! I haven't her things. Don't say a word about Melvina," vanished into the house.

"Come, Anna," called Rebecca reprovingly. "Father will come to look for us if you do not hasten. Why did not Luretta give you back your shoes and stockings?" she asked as Anna came slowly down the path. "It's a stupid game for her to keep them, I will say"; and she put a protecting arm across her sister's shoulder. "But do not feel bad, Dan, dear; she will bring then over before bedtime, if the storm holds off; and Mother has made a fine molasses cake for supper." But Anna made no response.

"Oh! Here comes the minister. Keep a little behind me, Dan, and he may not notice your bare feet," exclaimed Rebecca.

Usually the Reverend Mr. Lyon was very ceremonious in his greeting to the children of the parish; but to-night he wasted no time in salutations.

"Have you seen Melvina?" he asked anxiously. "She left home early this afternoon to visit at Captain Horton's and did not appear there at all; nor can we find trace of her."

"No, sir," responded Rebecca. "I have but come to fetch my sister home from Mr. Foster's, and have seen naught of Melvina."

Mr. Lyon turned and hurried back toward the main path, where London Atus was inquiring at every house if anyone had seen his little mistress; but no one had news of her.

"What can have befallen Melvina Lyon? And there's a storm coming up. I do hope no harm has come to her," said Rebecca, as she hurried Anna along the path.

"Oh, Rebby! It mustn't storm!" exclaimed Anna.

"'Twill only postpone Father's trip to the forest, Dan," said Rebby; "but look at those black clouds. 'Twill surely be a tempest. I hope we'll reach home before it breaks," and she started to run, pulling Anna along with her.

"Oh, Rebby, let me go! I can't go home! I can't!" exclaimed Anna, breaking away from her sister's clasping hand and darting ahead.

Rebecca had not heard Anna's last words, and thought her sister wished only to outrun her in the race home. So she ran quickly after her, and when at the turn by the blacksmith shop she lost sight of Anna she only thought that the younger girl was hidden by the turn of the path, and not until she pushed open the kitchen door did Rebecca realize that Anna had run away from her, that she had not meant to come home.

"Just in time," said Mr. Weston, drawing Rebecca in and closing the door against a gust of wind and rain. "But why did you not bring Danna home? It has set in for a heavy storm, and she will now have to stay the night at Mr. Foster's."

CHAPTER IV

AT MR. LYON'S

ANNA raced back along the path to the bluff as fast as she could go; but the strong wind swept against her, and at times nearly blew her over. The rain came down in torrents; and, as it had grown dark with the approaching storm, she could no longer see her way clearly, and stubbed her toes against roots and stones until her feet were hurt and bleeding.

But she could not stop to think of this: she could think only of Melvina, cowering, wet and afraid, under the juniper bushes.

"Perhaps she will be blown down the slope into the river," thought Anna, "and it will be my fault. Perhaps I have killed Melvina, by trying to make myself out as cleverer than she. Oh! If she is only safe I'll never try to be clever again," she vowed, as she fought her way on against wind and rain.

As she reached the top of the bluff there was a moment's lull in the storm, and Anna could clearly see the wide branched juniper bushes where she had left Melvina.

"Melly! Melly!" she called, scrambling down the slope. But there was no answer; and in a moment Anna realized that Melvina was not under the trees.

The storm began again with even greater violence, and Anna was obliged to cling closely to the rough branches to keep from being swept down the slope. She could hear the dash of the waves on the shore, and she trembled at the thought that Melvina might have been swept down into the angry waters.

After a little Anna, on her hands and knees, crawled up the slope, clinging to bits of grass here and there, and not venturing to stand upright until she had reached the top.

She knew what she must do now, and she did not hesitate. She must go straight to Mr. Lyon's house and tell him the story from the moment that she had told Melvina that pine trees were alders. For a moment she wondered what would become of her afterward; but only for a moment did she think of herself.

It seemed to the little girl that she would never reach the minister's house. For a moment she rested in the shelter of the church, and then dragged herself on. Her feet hurt so badly now that it was all she could do to walk.

There were lights to be seen, up-stairs and down, at the parsonage; but Anna did not wonder at this. She managed to reach the front door and to lift the knocker.

In a moment London opened the door, holding a candle above his head.

"Well, boy, who be ye?" he questioned sharply, seeing only Anna's curly brown head.

"If you please, I am Anna Weston," faltered the little girl. "I—I—must see the minister. It's about Melvina."

A smile showed on the black face, and London nodded his head.

"Missy Melvina am safe in bed," he whispered, then in a louder tone, "Step in, if ye please, Missy Anna."

Anna dragged herself up the high step, and Mr. Lyon just then opened a door leading into his study.

"What is it, London?" he questioned, and seeing Anna, lifted his hands in amazement.

Anna stumbled toward him.

"I am to blame about Melvina!" she exclaimed, and, speaking as quickly as she could, she told the whole story. She told it exactly as it had happened, excepting Luretta's part of the mischief, and Melvina's willingness to wade in the creeping tide.

Mr. Lyon had taken her by the hand and led her into the candle-lit room. A little fire blazed on the brick hearth, and as Anna came near it a little mist of steam rose from her wet clothes.

The minister listened, keeping Anna's cold little hand fast in his friendly clasp. His face was very grave, and when she finished with: "Is Melvina safe? London said she was. But, oh, Mr. Lyon, all her fine clothes are swept away, and it is my fault," he smiled down at her troubled face.

"Be in no further alarm, my child. But come with me, for your feet are cut and bruised, and Mrs. Lyon will give you dry clothing. Melvina does not blame you in her story of this mischievous prank. But I doubt not you are both blameworthy. But 'twill be your parents' duty to see to thy punishment." As the minister spoke he drew her toward a door at the far end of the room and opened it, calling for Mrs. Lyon, who rose from her seat near a low table in front of the big kitchen fireplace.

All Anna's courage had vanished. She hung her head, not daring to look at Mrs. Lyon, saying:

"I must go home. I must not stay."

"London is at your father's house ere this, and will tell him that you are to spend the night here. They will not be anxious about you," said Mrs. Lyon; "and now slip out of those wet garments. I have warm water to bathe your feet," and almost before Anna realized what was happening she found herself in a warm flannel wrapper, her bruised feet bathed and wrapped in comforting bandages, and a bowl of hot milk and corn bread on the little table beside her. When this was finished Mrs. Lyon led the little girl to a tiny chamber at the head of the stairs. A big bedstead seemed nearly to fill the room.

"Say your prayers, Anna," said Mrs. Lyon, and without another word she left the little girl alone. Anna was so thoroughly tired out that even the strange dark room did not prevent her from going to sleep, and when she awoke the tiny room was full of sunshine; she could hear robins singing in the maples near the house, and people moving about downstairs. Then she sat up in bed with a little shiver of apprehension.

What would the minister and Mrs. Lyon and Melvina say to her? Perhaps none of them would even speak to her. She had never been so unhappy in her life as she was at that moment. She slipped out of bed; but the moment her feet touched the floor she cried out with pain. For they were bruised and sore.

There was a quick rap at the door, and Mrs. Lyon entered. "Good-morning, Anna. Here are your clothes. I have pressed them. And I suppose these are your shoes and stockings!" and she set down the stout shoes and the knit stockings that Anna had supposed had been swept out to sea.

"When you are dressed come to the kitchen and your breakfast will be ready," said Mrs. Lyon, and left the room before Anna had courage to speak. Anna dressed quickly; but in spite of her endeavors she could not get on her shoes. Her feet hurt her too badly to take off the bandages; she drew her stockings on with some difficulty, and shoes in hand went slowly down the steep stairs.

When she was nearly down she heard Mrs. Lyon's voice: "She is a mischievous child, and her parents encourage her. She looks like a boy, and I do not want Melvina to have aught to do with her."

Anna drew a quick breath. She would not go into the kitchen and face people who thought so unkindly of her. "I will go home," she thought, ready to cry with the pain from her feet, and her unhappy thoughts. The front door was wide open. There was no trace of the storm of the previous night, and Anna made her way softly across the entry and down the steps. Every step hurt, but she hurried along and had reached the church when she gave a little cry of delight, for her father was coming up the path.

"Well, here's my Danna safe and sound," he exclaimed, picking her up in his arms. "And what has happened to her little feet?" he asked, as he carried her on toward home.

And then Anna told all her sad story again, even to the words she had overheard Mrs. Lyon say.

"Don't worry, Danna! I'd rather have my Dan than a dozen of their Melvinas," said Mr. Weston quickly.

When London had come the previous night with the brief message from the minister that Anna was safe at his house and would stay the night there, the Westons had been vexed and troubled, and Mrs. Weston had declared that Anna should be punished for running off in such a tempest to the minister's house. But as Mr. Weston listened to his little daughter's story, and looked at her troubled and tear-stained face, he decided that Anna had had a lesson that she would remember, and needed comforting more than punishment; and a few whispered words to Mrs. Weston, as he set Anna down in the big wooden rocker, made Anna's mother put her arms tenderly about her little daughter and say kindly:

"Mother's glad enough to have her Danna home again. And now let's look at those feet."

Rebby came running with a bowl of hot porridge, and the little girl was made as comfortable as possible. But all that morning she sat in the big chair with her feet on a cushion in a smaller chair, and she told her mother and Rebby all the story of her adventures; and when Rebby laughed at Melvina's not knowing an alder from a pine Danna smiled a little. But Mrs. Weston was very sober, although she said no word of blame. If Melvina Lyon's things had been lost it would be but right that Anna's parents should replace them to the best of their ability, and this would be a serious expense for the little household.

After dinner Rebby went to the Fosters', and came home with the story of Melvina's return home. It seemed that the moment Anna left her she became frightened and had followed her up the slope; and then, while Mr. Lyon and London were searching for her, she had made her way home, told her story, and had been put to bed. Luretta had carried Melvina's things and Anna's shoes and stockings well up the shore, and had put them under the curving roots of the oak tree; so, although they were well soaked, they were not blown away, and early that morning Luretta had hastened to carry the things to the parsonage.

"You were brave, Dan, to go through all that storm last night to tell the minister," said Rebby, as she drew a footstool near her sister's chair and sat down. Rebby was not so troubled to-day; for her father had postponed his trip to the forest after the liberty tree, and Rebby hoped that perhaps it would not be necessary that one should be set up in Machias. So she was ready to keep her little sister company, and try to make her forget the troubles of her adventures.

"Of course I had to go, Rebby," Anna responded seriously, "but none of it, not even my feet, hurt so bad as what Mrs. Lyon said about me. For I do not think I am what she said," and Anna began to cry.

"Father says you are the bravest child in the settlement; and Mother is proud that you went straight there and took all the blame. And I am sure that no other girl is so dear as my Danna," declared Rebby loyally. "After all, what harm did you do?"

But Anna was not so easily comforted. "I tried to make fun of Melly for not knowing anything. I tried to show off," she said, "and now probably she will never want to see me again; and oh, Rebby! the worst of it all is that Melvina is just as brave as she can be, and I like her!" And Anna's brown eyes brightened at the remembrance of Melvina's enjoyment of their sport together.

"Don't you worry, Danna; Father will make it all right," Rebecca assured her; for Rebecca thought that her father could smooth out all the difficult places.

Anna did not speak of the excursion to the forest; she did not even think of it until that evening, when her father came home with a roll of fine birch-bark, soft and smooth as paper, on whose smooth surface she and Rebecca with bits of charcoal could trace crude pictures of trees and Indians, of birds and mice, and sometimes write letters to Lucia Horton or Luretta Foster.

"You must take good care of your feet, Dan, for I must start after the liberty tree in a few days," said Mr. Weston, "and I want your company."

Anna's face brightened, but Rebecca looked troubled.

"Why must we have a liberty pole, Father?" she asked fretfully.

"We have good reasons, daughter. And to-day tidings have come that the brave men of Lexington and Concord, in Massachusetts, drove the British back to Boston on the nineteenth of April. 'Tis great news for all the colonies. I wish some British craft would give Machias men a chance to show their mettle," said Mr. Weston, his face flushing at the thought of the patriotic action of the men of Massachusetts.

Rebecca sighed. She, too, wished that her home town might do its part to win a victory for America; but, remembering what Lucia Horton had told her, the very mention of a liberty pole made her tremble.

When Anna hobbled up-stairs that night she was in a much happier frame of mind.

"My father is the best father in all the world, and my mother is the best mother, and my sister is the best sister," she announced to the little group as she said good-night. But the shadow of Mrs. Lyon's disapproval was not forgotten; Anna wondered to herself if there was not some way by which she could win the approval of Mr. and Mrs. Lyon, and so be allowed to become Melvina's friend.

"Mrs. Lyon doesn't like me because my hair is short, for one reason," thought Anna. "I'll let it grow; but 'twill take years and years," and with this discouraging thought her eyes closed, and she forgot her troubles in sleep.

CHAPTER V

A BIRTHDAY

In a few days Anna's feet were healed, and, wearing her soft moccasins, she could run about as well as ever. But her father and mother were quick to see that a great change had come over their little daughter. She no longer wanted to be called "Dan"; she told her mother that she wanted her hair to grow long, and she even asked Rebecca to teach her how to sew more evenly and with tinier stitches.

For Anna had made a firm resolve; she would try in every possible way to be like Melvina Lyon. She gave up so many of her out-of-door games that Mrs. Weston looked at her a little anxiously, fearing that the child might not be well. Every day Anna walked up the path to the church, and lingered about hoping for a glimpse of Melvina; but a week passed and the little girls did not meet.

At last the day came when Mr. Weston was ready to start for the forest to select the liberty tree; but, greatly to his surprise, Anna said that she did not wish to go, and he started off without her.

This was the first real sacrifice Anna had made

toward becoming like Melvina. She was quite sure that Melvina would not go for a tramp in the forest. "It would spoil her clothes," reflected Anna, and looked regretfully at her own stout gingham dress, wishing it could be changed and become like one of Melvina's dresses of flounced linen.

"I would look more like her if I wore better dresses," she decided.

"Mother, may I not wear my Sunday dress?" she asked eagerly. "I will not play any games, or hurt it. I will only walk as far as the church and back."

For a moment Mrs. Weston hesitated. It seemed a foolish thing to let Anna wear her best dress on a week day; but the little girl had been so quiet and unhappy since the night of her adventure that her mother decided to allow her this privilege; and Anna ran up-stairs, and in a few minutes had put on her Sunday dress. It was a blue muslin with tiny white dots, and the neck and sleeves were edged with tiny white ruffles. It had been Rebecca's best dress for several summers, until she outgrew it, and it was made over for the younger girl, but Anna was very proud of it, and stood on tiptoe to see herself reflected in the narrow mirror between the windows of the sitting-room. Her mother had made a sunbonnet of the same material as the dress, and Anna put this on with satisfaction. Always before this she had despised a sunbonnet, and never had she put it on of her own accord. But to-day she looked at it approvingly. "No one would know but that my hair is long, and braided, just like Melvina's," she thought as she walked slowly toward the kitchen.

"I will only walk to the church and straight back, Mother dear," she said, "and then I will put on my gingham dress, and sew on my patchwork."

"That's a good girl. You look fine enough for a party," responded her mother, and stood at the door watching Anna as she walked soberly down the path.

"I know not what has come over the child," she thought, with a little sigh. "To be sure, she is more like other little girls, and perhaps it is well"; but Mrs. Weston sighed again, as if regretting her noisy, singing "Dan," who seemed to have vanished forever.

When Anna reached the church she stood for a moment looking wistfully toward the parsonage. "If Mrs. Lyon could see me now she would not think me a tomboy," thought Anna; and with the thought came a new inspiration: why should not Mrs. Lyon see her dressed as neatly as Melvina herself, and with the objectionable short hair hidden from sight?

"I will go and call," decided Anna, her old courage returning; "and I will behave so well that Mrs. Lyon will ask me to come often and play with Melvina," and, quite forgetting to walk quietly, she raced along the path in her old-time fashion until she was at the minister's door. Then she rapped, and stood waiting, a little breathless, but smiling happily, quite sure that a little girl in so pretty a dress and so neat a sunbonnet would receive a warm welcome. Perhaps Mrs. Lyon would come to the door, she thought hopefully.

But it was Melvina herself who opened the door. Melvina, wearing a white dress and a long apron.

For a moment the two little girls stood looking at each other in surprise. Then Melvina smiled radiantly. "Oh! It really is you, Anna! Come in. I am keeping house this afternoon, and nobody will know that you are here."

"But I came to call on your mother. I wanted her to see me," explained Anna.

But Melvina did not seem to notice this explanation. She took Anna's hand and drew her into the house.

"Oh, Dan! wasn't it fun to wade and run on the shore?" said Melvina eagerly, as the two girls entered the big pleasant kitchen. "I didn't mind being wet or frightened or punished. Did you?"

"I wasn't punished," Anna responded meekly.

"I was. I was sent to bed without my supper for three nights; and I had to learn two tables of figures," declared Melvina triumphantly. "But I didn't care. For I have a splendid plan——" But before Melvina could say another word the kitchen door opened and Mrs. Lyon entered.

At first she did not recognize Anna, and smiled pleasantly at the neat, quiet little girl in the pretty dress and sunbonnet. "And who is this little maid?" she asked.

"I am Anna Weston" Anna replied quickly, making a clumsy curtsy.

Mrs. Lyon's smile vanished. She thought to herself that Anna had taken advantage of her absence to steal into the house, perhaps to entice Melvina for some rough game out-of-doors.

"I came to call," Anna continued bravely, her voice faltering a little. "I wanted to say I was sorry for being mischievous."

Mrs. Lyon's face softened, and she noticed approvingly that Anna's short curly locks were covered by the sunbonnet, and that she was dressed in her best; but she was still a little doubtful.

"Well, Anna, I am glad indeed that you are so right-minded. It is most proper that you should be sorry. I doubt not that your good parents punished you severely for your fault," said Mrs. Lyon. But she did not ask Anna to sit down, or to remove her sunbonnet. Melvina looked from Anna to her mother, not knowing what to say.

"I think I must go now," said Anna, almost ready to cry. "Good-bye, Melvina; good-afternoon, Mrs. Lyon," and making another awkward curtsy Anna turned toward the door.

"Oh, Danna! Don't go," called Melvina, running toward her; but Mrs. Lyon's firm hand held her back.

"Good-afternoon, Anna! I hope you will grow into a good and obedient girl," she said kindly.

Anna's tears now came thick and fast. She could hardly see the path as she stumbled along. But if she could have heard Melvina's words as her mother held her back from the kitchen door, she would have felt that her visit had been worth while. For Melvina had exclaimed, greatly to Mrs. Lyon's dismay: "Oh, Mother! Ask her to come again. For I want to be exactly like Danna, and do all the things she does."

Luretta Foster, coming down the path, stopped short and stared at Anna in amazement. It was surprising enough to see Anna dressed as if ready for church, but to see her in tears was almost unbelievable.

"What is the matter, Danna?" she asked, coming close to her little friend's side, and endeavoring to peer under the sunbonnet. "Would not your father let you go with him to the forest?"

Anna made no answer, and when Luretta put a friendly arm about her shoulders, she drew a little away.

"Do not cry, Dan. My brother Paul has gone to the forest with your father, and he promised to bring me home a rabbit to tame for a pet. I will give it to you, Dan," said Luretta.

For a moment Anna forgot her troubles. "Will you, truly, Luretta?" and she pushed back her sunbonnet that she might see her friend more clearly.

"Yes, I will. And I will give you a nice box with slats across the top, and a little door at the end that Paul made yesterday for the rabbit to live in," Luretta promised generously. "I do not suppose Melvina Lyon would know a rabbit from a wolf," she continued laughingly, quite sure that Anna would suggest asking Melvina to come and see their tame wolf. But Anna did nothing of the sort.

"Melvina knows more than any girl in this settlement," Anna replied quickly. "She can do sums in fractions, and she can embroider, and make cakes. And she is brave, too."

"Why, Dan Weston! And only last week you made fun of her, and said that all those things were of no account," exclaimed Luretta.

For a moment the two little friends walked on in silence, and then Anna spoke.

"Luretta, I'll tell you something. I am going to try to be exactly like Melvina Lyon. Everybody praises her, and your mother and mine are always saying that she is well-behaved. And I am going to let my hair grow long and be well-behaved. But don't tell anyone," Anna added quickly, "for I want Mrs. Lyon to find it out first of all."

"Oh, Dan! And won't you make funny rhymes any more? Or play on the timber-rafts—or—or—anything?" asked Luretta.

"I don't believe there is any harm in making rhymes. It's something you can't help," responded Anna thoughtfully. "And Parson Lyon has written a book," she added quickly, as if that in some way justified her jingles.

"I don't want you to be different, Dan!" declared Luretta.

Anna stopped and looked at her friend reproachfully. "Well, Luretta Foster, I am surprised!" she said, and then clasping Luretta's hand she started to run down the path, saying: "Let's hurry, so I can take off this dress; then we will walk a little way toward the forest to see if Father and Paul are coming. Will you truly give me the rabbit if Paul captures one?"

"Yes, I will," promised Luretta; but she began to wish that she had not suggested such a thing. If Danna was going to be exactly like Melvina Lyon, thought Luretta, a rabbit would not receive much attention.

Rebecca was sitting on the front step busy with her knitting as the two little girls came up the path. It was her birthday, but so far no one had seemed to remember it. The *Polly* had not reached port, so the fine present she had been promised could not be expected. But Rebecca was surprised and disappointed that everyone had seemed to forget that she was fourteen on the tenth of May. But as she looked up and saw Anna dressed in her best, and Luretta beside her, coming up the path, Rebby's face brightened. "I do believe Mother has planned a surprise for me," she thought happily. "Oh, there comes Lucia! Now I am sure that Mother has asked her to come, and perhaps some of the other girls," and Rebecca put down her knitting and stood up, smiling at the girls expectantly, for she was quite sure that their first words would be a birthday greeting.

At that moment Mrs. Weston, busy in her kitchen, remembered suddenly that it was May tenth. "My Rebby's birthday! And, with my mind full of all the worry about being shut off from the world by British cruisers, and provisions growing so scarce, I had forgotten," and Mrs. Weston left her work and reached the front door just as Rebecca rose to her feet to greet her friends.

"Fourteen to-day, Rebby dear," said Mrs. Weston, putting her arm about her tall daughter and kissing Rebecca.

At the same moment, hearing her mother's words, Anna ran forward calling out: "Rebby is fourteen to-day."

Luretta and Lucia were close behind her, and Rebecca found herself the centre of a smiling happy group, and for the moment quite forgot that she must do without the present from Boston that her father had promised her.

CHAPTER VI

LUCIA HAS A PLAN

"I HAVE brought you a birthday gift, Rebby,"said Lucia, who had been looking forward all day to the moment when she could give her friend the small package that she now handed her.

Rebecca received it smilingly, and quickly unwound the white tissue paper in which it was wrapped, showing a flat white box. Inside this box lay a pair of white silk mitts.

Rebecca looked at them admiringly, and even Mrs. Weston declared that very few girls could hope for a daintier gift; while Anna and Luretta urged Rebecca to try them on at once, which she was quite ready to do. They fitted exactly, and Lucia was as proud and happy as Rebecca herself that her gift was so praised and appreciated.

"They came from France," she said. "Look on the box, Rebby, and you will see 'Paris, France.' My father bought them of a Boston merchant, and I have a pair for myself."

"Are any more girls coming, Mother?" Rebecca asked as Mrs. Weston led the way to the living-room.

"No, my dear. And I only——" Mrs. Weston hesitated. She had started to say that she had only remembered Rebecca's birthday a few moments earlier; but she stopped in time, knowing it would cloud the afternoon's pleasure; and Rebecca, smiling and delighted with Lucia's gift, and sure that her mother had some treat ready for them, exclaimed:

"I do not mind now so much that the *Polly* has not arrived; for I could have no gift finer than a pair of silk mitts."

Anna had taken off her sunbonnet and was sitting on one of the low rush-bottomed chairs near a window. She was very quiet, reproaching herself in her thoughts that she had no gift for her sister. What could she give her? For little girls in revolutionary times, especially those in remote villages, had very few possessions of their own, and Anna had no valued treasure that might make a present. If she had remembered in time, she thought, she would have asked her mother to help her make a needle-book.

Suddenly she jumped up and ran across the room and kissed her sister, first on one cheek and then on the other, saying:

"If I had golden beads in strings,
I'd give you these, and other things.
But Rebby, dear, I've only this
To give to-day: a birthday kiss."

Lucia and Luretta were sure that Anna must have had her verse all ready to repeat; and even Rebecca, who knew that Anna rhymed words easily, thought that Anna had prepared this birthday greeting, and was very proud of her little sister. But at the words, "golden beads," a great hope came into Rebecca's heart. Perhaps that was what the *Polly* was bringing for her.

"I am to have a rabbit," said Anna happily. "What shall I name it?"

Lucia did not seem much interested in anything so ordinary as a rabbit, and had no suggestion to offer, and while Anna and Luretta were deciding this question Lucia whispered to Rebecca: "When I go home be sure and walk a little way; I want to tell you something important."

Rebby nodded smilingly. For the moment she had entirely forgotten the uncomfortable secret that Lucia had confided in her, and was thinking only that it was really a wonderful thing to have a fourteenth birthday.

While the four little girls were talking happily in the living-room, Mrs. Weston was trying to think up some sort of a birthday treat for them. There was no white sugar in the house, or, for that matter, in the entire settlement. But the Westons had a small store of maple sugar, made from the sap of the maple trees, and Mrs. Weston quickly decided that this should be used for Rebecca's birthday celebration. She hurried to the pantry, and when an hour later she opened the door and called the girls to the kitchen they all exclaimed with delight.

The round table was covered with a shining white cloth, and Mrs. Weston had set it with her fine blue plates, that she had brought from Boston when she came to Machias, and that were seldom used.

By each plate stood a lustre mug filled with milk, and in the centre of the table was a heart-shaped cake frosted with maple sugar.

"Oh, Mother! This is my very best birthday!" Rebecca declared happily, and as the other girls seated themselves at the table she stood with bowed head to say the "grace" of thanks before cutting her birthday cake.

Anna wished to herself that Melvina Lyon might have been one of the guests, and shared the delicious cake. She wondered just how Melvina would behave on such an occasion; and was so careful with her crumbs, and so polite in her replies to the other girls that Lucia and Rebecca began to laugh, thinking Anna was making believe for their amusement.

Before the little girls left the table Mr. Weston appeared at the kitchen door, and was quite ready to taste the cake, and again remind Rebecca of the gift the *Polly* was bringing.

"Let me whisper, Father," she responded, drawing his head down near her own. "It's *beads*!" she whispered, and when her father laughed she was sure she was right, and almost as happy as if the longed-for gift was around her neck.

"Well, Paul and I found the liberty tree," said Mr. Weston, "and I cut it down and trimmed it save for its green plume. Paul is towing it down-stream now; and when we set it up 'twill be a credit to the town."

Lucia rose quickly. "I must be going home," she said, a little flush coming into her cheeks. "I have enjoyed the afternoon very much," she added politely; for if Melvina Lyon was the smartest girl in the village no one could say that any of the other little girls ever forgot to be well-mannered.

Rebecca followed her friend to the door, and they walked down the path together, while Anna and Luretta questioned Mr. Weston eagerly as to Paul's success in capturing a rabbit, and were made happy with the news that he had secured two young rabbits, and that they were safe in the canoe which Paul was now paddling down the river, towing the liberty tree behind him.

Rebecca and Lucia had gone but a few steps when Lucia whispered: "We mustn't let them put up the liberty tree. Oh, Rebby, why didn't you try to stop your father going after it?"

"How could I?" responded Rebecca. "And when I said: 'Why must Machias have a liberty pole?' he was ill pleased with me, and said I must be loyal to America's rights. Oh, Lucia! are you sure that——"

But Lucia's hand was held firmly over Rebby's mouth. "Ssh. Don't speak it aloud, Rebby. For 'twould make great trouble for my father, in any case, if people even guessed that he knew the plans of the British. But I could not help hearing what he said to Mother the day he sailed. But, Rebby, we must do something so the liberty pole will not be set up."

"Can't we tell my father?" suggested Rebecca hopefully.

"Oh, Rebecca Weston! If your father knew what I told you he would do his best to have the liberty pole put up at once," declared Lucia.

"But I have a plan, and you must help me," she continued. "Paul Foster will bring the sapling close in shore near his father's shop, and it will rest there to-night; and when it is dark we must go down and cut it loose and push it out so that the current will take it down-stream, and the tide will carry it out to sea. Then, before they can get another one, the *Polly* will come sailing in and all will be well."

"Won't the British ship come if we do not put up the liberty pole?" asked Rebecca.

"There! You have said it aloud, Rebby!" whispered Lucia reprovingly.

"Not all of it; but how can we go out of our houses in the night, Lucia?" replied Rebecca, who had begun to think that perhaps Lucia's plan was the easiest way to save the village. For Lucia had told her friend that the *Polly*, of which Lucia's father was captain, and the sloop *Unity,* owned and sailed by a Captain Jones of Boston, would be escorted to Machias by an armed British ship; and if a liberty pole was set up the British would fire upon the town. So it was no wonder that Rebecca was frightened and ready to listen to Lucia's plan to avert the danger.

She did not know that her father and other men of the settlement were already beginning to doubt the loyalty of the two captains to America's cause.

"It will be easy enough to slip out when everybody is asleep," Lucia replied to Rebecca's question. "We can meet at Mr. Foster's shop. If I get there first I will wait, and if you get there before me you must wait. As near ten o'clock as we can. And then it won't take us but a few minutes to push the sapling out into the current. Just think, Rebby, we will save the town, and nobody will ever know it but just us two."

Rebby sighed. She wished that Lucia's father had kept the secret to himself. Besides, she was not sure that it was right to prevent the liberty pole from being set up. But that the town should be fired upon by a

British man-of-war, and everyone killed, as Lucia assured her, when it could be prevented by her pushing a pine sapling into the current of the river, made the little girl decide that she would do as Lucia had planned.

"All right. I will be there, at the blacksmith shop, when it strikes ten to-night," she agreed, and the friends parted.

Rebecca walked slowly toward home, forgetting all the joy of the afternoon; forgetting even that it was her fourteenth birthday, and that a string of gold beads for her was probably on board the *Polly*.

Paul Foster towed the fine sapling to the very place that Lucia had mentioned, and his father came to the shore and looked at it admiringly as he helped Paul make it secure. "It is safely fastened and no harm can come to it," Mr. Foster said after they had drawn the tree partly from the water. Paul drew his canoe up on the beach, and taking the rabbits in the stout canvas bag, started for home.

Anna and Luretta were both on the watch for him, and came running to meet him. Anna now wore her every-day dress of gingham, and in her eagerness to see the rabbits she had quite forgotten to try and behave like Melvina Lyon.

"Why, it is a pity to separate the little creatures," Paul declared, when Luretta told him that she had promised one to Anna. "See how close they keep together. And this box is big enough for them both.

And they are so young they must be fed very carefully for a time."

"I know what we can do," declared Anna; "my rabbit can live here until he is a little larger, and then my father will make a box for him and I can take him home."

Paul said that would do very well, and that Anna could come each day and learn how to feed the little creatures, and what they liked best to eat.

"But which one is to be mine? They are exactly alike," said Anna, a little anxiously. And indeed there was no way of telling the rabbits apart, so Anna and Luretta agreed that when the time came to separate them it would not matter which one Anna chose for her own.

At supper time Anna could talk of nothing but the rabbits, and had so much to say that her father and mother did not notice how silent Rebecca was.

The little household retired early, and by eight o'clock Rebecca was in bed, but alert to every sound, and resolved not to go to sleep. The sisters slept together, and in a few minutes Anna was sound asleep. Rebecca heard the clock strike nine, then very quietly she got out of bed and dressed. Her moccasins made no noise as she stepped cautiously along the narrow passage, and down the steep stairway. She lifted the big bar that fastened the door and stood it against the wall, then she opened the door, closing it carefully behind her, and stepped out into the warm darkness of the spring night.

"BUT WHICH ONE IS TO BE MINE?"

CHAPTER VII

"A TRAITOR'S DEED"

It was one of those May evenings that promise that summer is close at hand. The air was soft and warm; there was no wind, and in the clear starlight Rebecca could see the shadows of the tall elm tree near the blacksmith shop, and the silvery line of the softly flowing river. As she stood waiting for Lucia she looked up into the clear skies and traced the stars forming the Big Dipper, nearly over her head. Low down in the west Jupiter shone brightly, and the broad band of shimmering stars that formed the Milky Way stretched like a jeweled necklace across the heavens. The little village slept peacefully along the river's bank; not a light was to be seen in any of the shadowy houses. A chorus of frogs from the marshes sounded shrilly through the quiet. In years to come, when Rebecca heard the first frogs sounding their call to spring, she was to recall that beautiful night when she stole out to try and save the town, as she believed, from being fired on by a British gunboat.

She had made so early a start that she had to wait what seemed a very long time for Lucia, who approached so quietly that not until she touched Rebby's arm did Rebby know of her coming.

"I am late, and I nearly had to give up coming because Mother did not get to sleep," Lucia explained, as the two girls hurried down to the river. "She is so worried about Father," continued Lucia; "she says that since the Americans defeated the English at Lexington they may drive them out of Boston as well."

"Of course they will," declared Rebecca, surprised that anyone could imagine the righteous cause of America defeated. "And if the English gunboat comes in here the Machias men will capture it," she added.

"Well, I don't know," responded Lucia despondently. "But if it destroyed the town there wouldn't be anyone left to capture it; and that is why we must push that liberty tree offshore."

The girls were both strong, and Lucia had brought a sharp knife with which to cut the rope holding the tree to a stake on the bank, so it did not take them long to push the tree clear of the shore. They found a long pole near by, and with this they were able to swing the liberty tree out until the current of the river came to their aid and carried it slowly along.

"How slowly it moves," said Rebecca impatiently, as they stood watching it move steadily down-stream.

"But it will be well down the bay before morning," said Lucia, "and we must get home as quickly as we can. I wish my father could know that there will not be a liberty pole set up in Machias."

Rebecca stopped short. "No liberty pole, Lucia Horton? Indeed there will be. Why, my father says that all the loyal settlements along the Maine coast are setting up one; and as soon as the old British gunboat is out of sight Machias will put up a liberty tree. Perhaps 'twill even be set up while the gunboat lies in this harbor."

"Well, come on! We have tried to do what we could to save the town, anyway," responded Lucia, who began to be sadly puzzled. If a liberty tree was so fine a thing why should her father not wish Machias to have one, she wondered. Lucia did not know that her father was even then bargaining with the British in Boston to bring them a cargo of lumber on his next trip from Machias, in return for permission to load the *Polly* with provisions to sell to the people of the settlement, and that, exactly as Lucia had heard him predict, an armed British gunboat would accompany the sloops *Polly* and *Unity* when they should appear in Machias harbor.

The two friends whispered a hasty "good-night," and each ran in the direction of home. Rebby pushed the big door open noiselessly, but she did not try to replace the bar. As she crept up the stairs she could hear the even breathing of her father and mother, and she slid into bed without waking Anna, and was too sleepy herself to lie long awake.

The unfastened door puzzled Mr. Weston when he came down-stairs at daybreak the next morning. "I was sure I put the bar up," he thought, but he had no time to think much about trifles that morning, for, as he stood for a moment in the doorway, he saw Paul Foster running toward the house.

"Mr. Weston, sir, the liberty pole is gone," gasped the boy, out of breath. "The rope that held it to the stake was cut," he continued. "Father says 'tis some Tory's work."

Mr. Weston did not stop for breakfast. He told Mrs. Weston that he would come up later on, as soon as he had found out more about the missing liberty tree; and with Paul beside him, now talking eagerly of how his father had gone with him to take a look at the pine sapling and found no trace of it, Mr. Weston hurried toward the shore where a number of men were now gathered.

Anna had hard work to awaken Rebby that morning, and when she came slowly down-stairs she felt cross and tired; but her mother's first words made her forget everything else.

"We will eat our porridge without your father," Mrs. Weston said gravely. "A terrible thing has happened. Some traitor has made way with the liberty tree that your father and Paul selected yesterday."

"Traitor?" gasped Rebby, who knew well that such a word meant the lowest and most to be despised person on earth, and could hardly believe that what she had supposed to be a fine and brave action could be a traitor's deed.

"Who else but a traitor would make way with our liberty pole?" responded Mrs. Weston. "But do not look so frightened, Rebby. Sit up to the table; when your father comes home he will tell us who did the base act. And we may be sure Machias men will deal with him as he deserves."

But Rebecca could not eat the excellent porridge; and when her mother questioned her anxiously she owned that her head ached, and that she did not feel well.

"I'll steep up some thoroughwort; a good cup of herb tea will soon send off your headache," said Mrs. Weston, "and you had best go back to bed. Maybe 'tis because of the birthday cake."

Rebecca made no response; she was glad to go back to her room, where she buried her face in the pillow, hardly daring to think what would become of her. Supposing Lucia should tell, she thought despairingly, saying over and over to herself, "Traitor! Traitor!" So that when Anna came softly into the room a little later she found her sister with flushed face and tear-stained eyes, and ran back to the kitchen to tell her mother that Rebby was very ill.

It was an anxious and unhappy morning for Rebby and for her mother, for Mrs. Weston became worried at the sight of her daughter's flushed cheeks and frightened eyes. She decided that it was best for Rebecca to remain in bed; and, had it not been for the frequent doses of bitter herb tea which her mother insisted on her drinking, Rebby would have been well satisfied to hide herself away from everyone.

Anna helped her mother about the household work, thinking to herself that probably Melvina Lyon was doing the same. After the dishes had been washed and set away Mrs. Weston suggested that Anna should run down to Luretta Foster's.

"'Twill be best to keep the house quiet this morning, and you can see the rabbits," she added.

"But, Mother! I am not noisy. Do I not step quietly, and more softly?" pleaded Anna. She was quite ready to run off to her friend's, but she was sure her mother must notice that she was no longer the noisy girl who ran in and out of the house singing and laughing.

"Well, my dear child, you have been 'Anna,' not 'Dan,' for a week past. And I know not what has turned you into so quiet and well-behaved a girl," responded her mother. "But run along, and be sure and inquire if there be any news of the rascal who made way with the liberty tree."

Anna started off very sedately, measuring her steps and holding her head a little on one side as she had noticed that Melvina sometimes did. She was thinking of Rebby, and what a pity it was to have to stay indoors when the sun was so warm, and when there were so many pleasant things to do. "I will go over on the hill and get her some young checkerberry leaves," resolved Anna, remembering how Rebby liked their sharp flavor. Then she remembered that the rabbits were to be named that morning; and, forgetting all about Melvina, she ran swiftly along the path, beginning to sing in her old-time manner.

Luretta was watching for her, and smiled happily when she heard Anna's voice. "Oh! She's going to stay 'Danna,' and not be like that stuck-up Melvina Lyon," she thought with delight; for Luretta did not think Anna would make a satisfactory playmate if she were going to change into a quiet, well-behaved girl like the minister's little daughter.

In a few minutes the girls were beside the box that held the captive rabbits, who looked up at them with startled eyes. Paul had brought a basket of fresh grass, and some bits of tender bark and roots on which the little creatures were nibbling.

"I do wish they were not exactly alike," said Anna.

But Luretta declared that she thought it was much better that way. "Because I should want you to have the prettiest one, and you would want me to have the prettiest one, and how could we ever choose?" she explained; and Anna acknowledged that perhaps it was better that the rabbits should be alike in every way. After much discussion of names they decided that the rabbits must be called as nearly alike as possible; and so the new pets were named "Trit" and "Trot."

Every little child in the neighborhood enjoyed a visit at Luretta's home. In the first place because of Mrs. Foster's pleasant smile and kind welcome, and also because of the wonderful treasures it contained. There was a great round ostrich egg, which Mr. Foster's brother had brought from far-off Africa. This egg was carefully kept in a wooden box on the high mantel shelf; but Mrs. Foster was never too busy to take it down and let the little visitor gaze at it with admiring eyes. Then there was a model of a water-mill, with its tiny wheels, as complete as if it could begin work at once. This stood on a table in the corner of the sitting-room, where anyone might stand and admire it, and hear Luretta or Paul tell that their father had made every bit of it himself. Besides these treasures Mrs. Foster, with a pair of scissors and a bit of paper, could make the most beautiful paper dolls that any little girl could wish to possess; and whenever Luretta's friends came for a visit they usually took home a paper doll, or perhaps a bird cut from paper, or a horse. So Anna was ready to leave even the beautiful rabbits and go indoors. But this morning Mrs. Foster did not seem her usual cheerful self.

"This is sad news about our liberty tree; but the men have set out in boats to search for it, and 'twill be a good omen indeed if they find and bring it back," she said.

"My father says 'twill be a great day for the settlement when 'tis put up," said Anna, looking longingly toward the box on the high mantel, and hoping she might have a look at the wonderful egg.

"And so it will be. With Boston in the hands of the British, and no safety on land or sea 'tis time each town showed some mark of loyalty," declared Mrs. Foster. "I will put on my sunbonnet and we will walk to the wharves, and perhaps hear some news of the traitor who made way with it. I said at first maybe 'twas the mischief of some boy who did not realize what the tree stood for; but Paul flared up at once and said there was no boy on the coast of Maine who would do such a thing, unless 'twas a young Tory; and we know of no Tory here."

As they neared the wharf they heard a loud cheer from a group of men, and could see that a boat, rowed by Mr. Weston and Mr. Foster, was coming rapidly toward the shore and behind it trailed the fine pine sapling.

"And there comes Parson Lyon with his little daughter," said Mrs. Foster. "He is as good a patriot as General Washington himself," she added admiringly.

As Mr. Lyon came near the little group he stopped for a moment.

"May I leave my daughter with you?" he asked. "I wish to be one of those who lift that sacred tree to safety." And he hurried on to the wharf, leaving Melvina, who stood smiling delightedly at this unexpected meeting with Anna.

CHAPTER VIII

"WHITE WITCHES"

FOR a moment both Anna and Luretta looked at Melvina a little doubtfully, for they could but remember and be ashamed of their part in the foolish game they had tried to play with her so short a time ago. But Melvina was smiling and friendly, and evidently had cherished no ill-feeling toward them. By the time she had replied to Mrs. Foster's friendly inquiries in regard to her mother, Anna and Luretta were quite at their ease; and Luretta said to herself that she did not wonder Anna wanted to be like Melvina. Luretta even began to wonder if it would not be well for her to learn to speak as softly as did Melvina Lyon; it certainly had a pleasant sound, she thought admiringly.

"I must return home," said Mrs. Foster, "but Melvina's father will expect her to wait here for him; so, Luretta, you and Anna may stay with her until he comes. Here is a clean log where you can sit comfortably, and do not go far from this spot."

The little girls promised, and Mrs. Foster started for home. Hardly had she turned her back when Melvina clasped Anna by the hand, and exclaimed: "Now you can tell me more about the woods, and the little animals who live in hollow logs or burrow under rocks, and about the different birds and their nests! Oh, begin quickly, for my father may soon return," and she drew Anna toward the big log that lay near the path.

"Tell her about our rabbits, Danna," suggested Luretta. "My brother Paul brought me two little gray rabbits from the forest," she explained; and Melvina listened eagerly to the description of Trit and Trot, and of their cunning ways and bright eyes, and was told that they had already lost their fear of Luretta and Anna.

"I wish I could see them. I have never seen any little animals except kittens," said Melvina. It seemed to Melvina that Anna and Luretta were very fortunate children. They could run about in old clothes, play on the shore and among the piles of lumber, and they knew many strange and interesting things about the creatures of the forest which she had never before heard. The long lessons that she had to learn each morning, the stint of neat stitches that she had to set each day, and the ceremonious visits now and then, when she always had to take her knitting, and was cautioned by her anxious mother to "remember that she was a minister's daughter, and behave properly, and set a good example"—all these things flitted through

Melvina's thoughts as tiresome tasks that she would like to escape, and be free as Anna seemed to be.

"Mayn't I bring the rabbits down here for Melvina to see?" asked Anna. "The box would not be very heavy."

But Luretta had objections to this plan. Her brother had told her not to move the box from the sunny corner near the shed; and, beside this, she was sure it was too heavy for Anna to lift. "If you should let it fall they might get out and run away," she concluded. Then, noticing Anna's look of disappointment, she added: "I know what you may do, Danna. You and Melvina may go up and see the rabbits, and I will wait here for Parson Lyon and tell him where Melvina is, and that we will see her safely home; and then I will hurry after you."

"Oh! Yes, indeed; that is a splendid plan," said Melvina eagerly, jumping up from the log. "Let us go now, Anna. And is not Luretta kind to think of it?"

Anna agreed rather soberly. Mrs. Foster had told them to remain near the log, she remembered, but if Melvina saw no harm in Luretta's plan she was sure it must be right; so taking Melvina's hand they started off.

"Let's run, Anna," urged Melvina; for Anna was walking sedately, in the manner in which she had so often seen Melvina come down the path, and she was a little surprised that her companion had not at once noticed it. But Anna was always ready to run, and replied quickly: "Let's race, and see who can get to the blacksmith shop first."

Away went the two little girls, Melvina's long braids dancing about, and her starched skirts blown back as she raced along; and, greatly to Anna's surprise, Melvina passed her and was first at the shop.

"I beat! I beat!" exclaimed Melvina, her dark eyes shining and her face flushed with the unwonted exercise.

"You do everything best," Anna declared generously, "but I did not know that you could run so fast."

"Neither did I," Melvina acknowledged laughingly. Anna felt a little puzzled by this sudden change in Melvina, which was far more noticeable than Anna's own effort to give up her boyish ways and become a quiet, sedate little girl. For ever since the few hours of freedom on the shore, on the day of the tempest, Melvina had endeavored to be as much like Anna as possible. She ran, instead of walking slowly, whenever she was out of her mother's sight. She had even neglected her lessons to go out-of-doors and watch a family of young robins one morning, and had been immediately called in by her surprised mother. In fact, Melvina had tried in every way to do things that she imagined Anna liked to do. She had even besought her mother to cut off her hair; but, as she dared not give her reason for such a wish, Mrs. Lyon had reproved her sharply, saying that it was a great misfortune for a little girl not to have smoothly braided hair, or long curls. So while Anna endeavored to cover her pretty curly hair, to behave sedately, and give up many of her outdoor games, in order to be like Melvina, Melvina was wishing that she could be exactly like Anna; and as they stood looking at each other at the end of their race each little girl noticed a change in the other which she could not understand, and they started off toward Luretta's home at a more sober pace.

"Here they are," said Anna, as they came to the corner of the shed and saw the rabbits looking out at them between the slats of the box.

Melvina kneeled down close to the box and exclaimed admiringly as Trit and Trot scurried away to the farthest corner.

"I do wish I could touch one! Would it not be fun to dress them up like dolls!" she said. "If they were mine I would dress them up in bonnets and skirts, and teach them to bow. Oh, Anna! Can't we take one out? One of them is yours, Luretta said so; let us take out your rabbit, Anna."

"But we haven't anything to dress it up in," said Anna, beginning to think that Melvina was a good deal like other little girls after all.

"Could we not take your rabbit over to my house, Anna? My mother has gone to Mrs. Burnham's to spend the day, and we could take Trot up to my room and dress her up and play games. Do, Anna!" urged Melvina.

"It would be great sport indeed," agreed Anna eagerly; "we could call Trot by some fine name, like Queen Elizabeth, and have your dolls for visitors."

"Yes, yes, we could! Or play Trot was a lion that we had captured in Africa. Where is the door to the box, Anna?" and Melvina's dark eyes shone more brightly than ever as Anna slid back the little door that Paul had so carefully made, and, after several vain efforts, finally secured one of the rabbits and quickly wrapped it in the skirt of her dress.

"Shut the door, Melvina! Quick! or the other will run out," she said, but although Melvina hastened to obey she was only just in time to catch the second rabbit in her hands; an instant later and it would have scampered away free.

"Put your skirt around it. Hurry, and let's run. Mrs. Foster is coming," whispered Anna, and the two little girls ran swiftly behind the shed, holding the trembling frightened rabbits, and then across the fields toward Mr. Lyon's house. Not until they reached the back door of the parsonage did either of them remember Luretta, and then it was Anna who exclaimed:

"But what will Luretta think when she comes home and does not find us, and sees the empty box?"

"She won't go home for a long time; we will be back and the rabbits safe in their box by that time," declared Melvina. "We will go up the back stairs, Anna; and we need not be quiet, for London has gone fishing. We will have a fine time! Oh, Anna, I am so glad you stopped me that day when we went wading, for now we are friends," she continued, leading the way up-stairs.

"But I was horrid, Melvina," Anna said, recalling her efforts to make Melvina appear silly and ignorant so that Luretta would scorn her.

"No, indeed, you were not," responded Melvina. "When we played on the shore you made me laugh and run. I never played like that before."

"Well, I think you are real good," said Anna humbly, as she followed Melvina into a pleasant sunny chamber. "Most girls would have been angry when their fine clothes were spoiled; and you were punished too, and I was not"; and Anna looked at Melvina admiringly, thinking to herself that she would do anything that Melvina could ask to make up to her for that undeserved punishment.

"You will have to hold both the rabbits while I get my dolls," said Melvina; and Anna's attention was fully occupied in keeping the two little creatures safe and quiet in the folds of her skirt, which she held together bag fashion, while Melvina drew a large box from the closet and took out three fine dolls.

Anna gazed at the dolls admiringly. Each one wore a gown of blue silk, and little shirred bonnets to match. Melvina explained that they, the dolls, all wanted to dress just alike.

"We will put these on Trit and Trot," she said, drawing out two white skirts from her collection of doll clothes. "And see these little white bonnets!" and she held up two tiny round bonnets of white muslin; "these will be just the thing."

The rabbits submitted to being dressed. Both the girls were very gentle with them, and gradually the little creatures grew less frightened. Neither Anna nor Melvina had ever had such delightful playthings before. The rabbits were Queen Elizabeth and Lady Washington, and the dolls came to bow low before them. The time passed very rapidly, and not until London was seen coming toward the house to prepare the noonday meal did the little girls give another thought to Luretta. Melvina, glancing from the window, saw London coming up the path with his basket of fish. She was holding Lady Washington, and for a second her clasp was less firm, and that was enough. With a leap the rabbit was through the open window, the white skirt fluttering about it. Anna, starting up in surprise, let go Queen Elizabeth, who followed Lady Washington through the window so closely that it was small wonder that London dropped his basket of fish and ran back a few steps with a loud cry. After a few scrambling leaps the rabbits disappeared, and London, trembling with fright, for he believed that the strange leaping creatures dressed in white must be some sort of evil witches, picked up his basket, and shaking his head and muttering to himself, came slowly toward the house.

"And there comes my father, and Luretta is with him," exclaimed Melvina. "What shall we do, Anna? And what will Luretta say when we tell her about the rabbits? Come, we must be at the front door when they get here, or my father will fear I am lost."

Mr. Lyon smiled as he saw his little girl standing in the doorway, and his troubled look vanished. But Luretta looked flushed and angry. All the morning she had been sitting on the log waiting for Mr. Lyon, and when he came at last she had hurried home only to find that her mother had not seen either of the girls, and Luretta had run after Mr. Lyon to tell him this, and accompanied him to the door.

"I will walk home with Luretta," Anna said with unusual meekness. Melvina watched them go, a little frightened at the end of the morning's fun. She did not know what they could say to Luretta to explain their mischief. At that moment London came into the front entry.

"I'se seen strange sights this mornin', massa!" he said, rolling his eyes. "I'se seen white witches flyin' out ob dis house."

"London! Do not talk of such wickedness," said Mr. Lyon sharply. "Even your little mistress is amused at such absurd talk," for Melvina, knowing what London had seen, was laughing heartily. But London, shaking his head solemnly, went back to the kitchen, sure that he had seen a strange and awful sight, and resolved to speak to Mr. Lyon again of the matter.

"Well, Danna Weston! You can't have one of my rabbits now, after treating me this way," said Luretta. "And I am not going to walk home with you, either," and she ran swiftly ahead.

Anna did not hurry after her, as Luretta hoped and expected. She began to feel very unhappy. Trit and Trot were gone, and who could tell but the skirts and bonnets might not strangle them? Then, suddenly, she remembered that Rebecca was at home ill, and that she had entirely forgotten her, and the young checkerberry leaves she had intended picking for her sister. She put the thought that it was all Melvina's fault out of her mind. Even if it were, had not she, Anna, led Melvina into a more serious trouble on the day of the tempest? She resolved that she would take all the blame of the lost rabbits, that Melvina should not even be questioned about them if she could help it. But it was a very sober little girl who went up the path toward home.

CHAPTER IX

REBECCA'S VISIT

BEFORE Anna reached home Rebecca had decided that she must see Lucia Horton as soon as possible; for she began to fear that Lucia in some way might betray their secret; but Rebecca knew that her mother would not consent to her going out until she appeared more like her usual self than she had at breakfast time. So she brushed her hair neatly, bathed her face, and just before Anna's return home, came into the kitchen.

"My head does not ache at all, Mother," she announced, "and I feel as well as ever."

Mrs. Weston looked at Rebby in astonishment. "I declare!" she exclaimed, "if thoroughwort tea doesn't beat all! But I never knew it to act as quickly before. Well, I must take time and go to the swamp for a good supply of it before this month goes. 'Tis best when gathered in May."

"May I not walk over and see Lucia?" Rebby asked a little fearfully, wondering what she could do if her mother refused.

"Why, yes; it will very likely do you good. But walk slowly, dear child," responded Mrs. Weston, taking

Rebecca's sunbonnet from its peg behind the door and tying the strings under Rebby's round chin.

"When the *Polly* comes into harbor you will have the gold beads from your Grandmother Weston, in Boston; but how Danna guessed it is more than I can imagine," she said, and Rebecca started down the path. Mrs. Weston stood for a moment in the doorway looking after her. She was more disturbed by Rebecca's sudden illness than she wished to acknowledge.

"I wish indeed that the *Polly* and *Unity* would come; perchance it is the lack of proper food that ails the children: too much Indian meal, and no sweets or rice or dried fruits," she thought anxiously. "And to think 'tis England, our own kinsfolk, who can so forget that we learned what justice and loyalty mean from England herself," she said aloud, as she returned to her household duties. For Mrs. Weston, like so many of the American colonists, had been born in an English village, and knew that the trouble between England and her American colonies was caused by the injustice of England's king, and his refusal to listen to wise advisers.

Lucia Horton's home lay in an opposite direction from the blacksmith shop. It stood very near the shore, and from its upper windows there was a good view of the harbor. It had no yard or garden in front, as did so many of the simple houses of the settlement, and the front door opened directly on the rough road which led along the shore.

Rebecca rapped on the door a little timidly, and when Mrs. Horton opened it and said smilingly: "Why, here is the very girl I have been wanting to see. Come right in, Rebecca Flora," she was rather startled.

"Lucia is not very well," Mrs. Horton continued, "and she has been saying that she must, *must* see Rebecca Flora; so it is most fortunate that you have arrived. Some great secret, I suppose," and Mrs. Horton smiled pleasantly, little imagining how important the girls' secret was. Her two elder sons, boys of fifteen and seventeen, were on the *Polly* with their father, and she and Lucia were often alone.

Rebecca had but stepped into the house when she heard her name called from the stairway. "Oh, Rebecca, come right up-stairs," called Lucia, and Mrs. Horton nodded her approval. "Yes, run along. 'Twill do Lucia good to see you. I cannot imagine what ails her to-day. I saw one of the O'Brien boys passing just now, and he tells me their liberty tree has been found and brought to shore!"

"Oh!" exclaimed Rebecca in so surprised a tone that Mrs. Horton laughed. " 'Twould have been full as well if the tree had been allowed to drift out to sea," she added in a lower tone.

Rebecca went up-stairs so slowly that Lucia called twice before her friend entered the chamber where

Lucia, bolstered up in bed, and with flushed cheeks and looking very much as Rebby herself had looked an hour earlier, was waiting for her.

"Shut the door tightly," whispered Lucia, and Rebecca carefully obeyed, and then tiptoed toward the bed.

For a moment the two girls looked at each other, and then Lucia whispered: "What will become of us, Rebecca? Mr. O'Brien told Mother that the men were determined to find out who pushed the liberty tree afloat, and that no mercy would be shown the guilty. That's just what he said, Rebby, for I heard him," and Lucia began to cry.

"But the tree is found and brought back," said Rebecca, "and how can anyone ever find out that we did it? No one will know unless we tell; and you wouldn't tell, would you, Lucia?"

Lucia listened eagerly, and gradually Rebecca grew more courageous, and declared that she was not at all afraid; that is, if Lucia would solemnly promise never to tell of their creeping down to the shore and cutting the rope that held the tree to the stake.

"Of course I never would tell," said Lucia, who was now out of bed and dressing as rapidly as possible. "I wasn't ill; but I stayed up-stairs because I was afraid you might tell," she confessed; and then Rebecca owned that she had felt much the same. "But I had to take a big bowlful of bitter thoroughwort tea," she added, making a little face at the remembrance.

"Well, you are a better medicine than thorough-wort tea," said Lucia; and Mrs. Horton opened the door just in time to hear this.

"Why, it is indeed so," she said, looking in surprise at her little daughter, who seemed quite as well as usual. "Your father has just passed, Rebecca, and I asked his permission for you to stay to dinner with us, and he kindly agreed. I think now I must have a little celebration that Lucia has recovered so quickly," and with a smiling nod she left the two girls.

"I know what that means," declared Lucia, for the moment forgetting the danger of discovery. "It means that we shall have rice cooked with raisins, and perhaps guava jelly or sugared nuts."

Rebecca looked at her friend as if she could hardly believe her own ears; for the dainties that Lucia named so carelessly were seldom enjoyed in the remote settlement; and although Captain Horton took care that his own pantry was well supplied it was not generally known among his neighbors how many luxuries his family enjoyed.

"Surely you are but making believe," said Rebecca.

"No, truly, Rebby; we will likely have all those things to-day, since Mother said 'twould be a celebration; and I am glad indeed that you are here. You do not have things like that at your house, do you?" said Lucia.

Rebecca could feel her cheeks flush, but she did not know why she felt angry at what Lucia had said.

It was true that the Westons, like most of their neighbors, had only the plainest food, but she wished herself at home to share the corn bread and baked fish that would be her mother's noon-day meal. She was silent so long that Lucia looked at her questioningly; and when Mrs. Horton called them to dinner they went down-stairs very quietly.

The table was set with plates of shining pewter. There was a loaf of white bread, now but seldom seen in the settlement, and a fine omelet; and, even as Lucia had said, there was boiled rice with raisins in it, and guava jelly.

Rebecca was hungry, and here was a treat spread before her such, as Lucia had truly said, she never had at home; but to Mrs. Horton's surprise and Lucia's dismay, Rebecca declared that she must go home; and taking her sunbonnet, with some stammering words of excuse she hastened away.

"A very ill-bred child," declared Mrs. Horton, "and I shall be well pleased if your father can take us away from this forsaken spot on his next trip."

Lucia sat puzzled and half frightened at Rebecca's sudden departure. Lucia did not for a moment imagine that anything she had said could have sent Rebecca flying from the house.

Mr. and Mrs. Weston and Anna were nearly through dinner when Rebecca appeared, and Mrs. Weston declared herself well pleased that Rebby had come home; there were no questions asked, and it seemed to Rebby that nothing had ever tasted better than the corn bread and the boiled fish; she had not a regretful thought for the Hortons' dainties.

Anna told the story of all that had occurred to her that morning; of taking the rabbits to the parsonage, and of London's exclamation and terror at the "white witches," and last of all of Luretta's anger. "And I didn't even tell Luretta that the rabbits were lost," concluded the little girl, and then, with a deep sigh, she added: "I suppose I will have to go right over and tell her."

"Yes," replied her mother gravely, "you must go at once. And you must tell Luretta how sorry you are for taking the rabbits from the box. And fail not to say to Mrs. Foster that you are ashamed at not keeping your promise."

Mr. Weston did not speak, but Rebecca noticed that he seemed pleased rather than vexed with his little daughter. "That's because Anna always tells everything," thought Rebecca. "But if I should tell what I did last night he would think me too wicked to forgive," and at the thought she put her head on the table and began to cry.

"Why, Rebby, dear! 'Tis my fault in letting you go out this morning," exclaimed Mrs. Weston, now quite sure that Rebecca was really ill. But in a few moments her tears ceased, and she was ready to help with washing the dishes and setting the room in order.

"I will walk along with you, Danna," said her father, when Anna was ready to start on the unpleasant errand of owning her fault to Luretta, and they started out together, Anna holding fast to her father's hand.

"I wish I need not go, Father," Anna said as they walked along.

Mr. Weston's clasp on his little daughter's hand tightened. "Let me see; do you not remember the verse from the Bible that 'he who conquers his own spirit is braver than he who taketh a city'?" he questioned gently.

Anna looked up at him wonderingly, and Mr. Weston continued: "It is your courage in owning your fault that makes you a conqueror, and as brave as a brave soldier."

"As brave as Washington?" asked Anna, and when her father smiled down at her she smiled back happily. Probably a little girl could not be as brave as a great soldier, she thought, but if her father was pleased it would not be so hard, after all, to tell Luretta about Trit and Trot. But Anna again firmly resolved that she would take all the blame herself; Melvina should not be blamed in any way for the loss of the rabbits.

CHAPTER X

AN AFTERNOON WALK

At the turn by the blacksmith shop Mr. Weston said good-bye, and Anna went on alone to Luretta's home. The front door was open, and before she reached the house she heard someone crying, and when she stood on the door-step she realized that it was Luretta, and that Mrs. Foster was endeavoring to comfort her.

"The rabbits are much happier to be free to run back to the woods. Perhaps by this time they have found their mother, and are telling all their adventures to their brothers and sisters," she heard Mrs. Foster say.

"But Danna and Melvina may have taken them," sobbed Luretta; and then Anna rapped at the door.

"Come in," called Mrs. Foster, and Anna, a little timidly, entered the sitting-room.

Luretta looked up, but did not speak.

"Come right in, Anna," said Mrs. Foster pleasantly. "Luretta has bad news for you; the rabbits are gone."

Anna did not look up, and there was an uncomfortable silence for a moment. Then she began her story:

"If you please, Mistress Foster, I am sorry I broke my promise to you this morning. You bade me to wait with Melvina by the big log, and I did not."

"You came and took my rabbits," wailed Luretta, "and I s'pose you gave one to that stuck-up Melvina."

Anna nodded. "Yes, I did take them; but I meant to bring them back, Luretta, truly I did. But they got away."

A fresh wail from Luretta made Anna look pleadingly up at Mrs. Foster, whose eyes rested kindly upon her.

"Luretta, stop thy foolish crying," said Mrs. Foster, "and let Anna tell you all the story of the rabbits." Then she rested her hand on Anna's shoulder and said kindly:

"I am glad, Anna, that you and Luretta are friends, for thou art a brave and honest child. Now, I must attend to my work, and I will leave you," and the two little girls found themselves alone in the room.

Luretta was sitting in the big cushioned wooden rocker, with her face hidden against the back. Anna was standing in front of her, trying to think of something to say that would make Luretta forgive her. Then she heard Luretta's half-smothered voice say: "Do you s'pose our rabbits did find their mother?"

"I don't know, Luretta, but I only meant to let Melvina play with them. We—I took them out and carried them over to Melvina's house and we dressed them up in doll's clothes——"

"Yes? Yes? And what else?" asked Luretta eagerly, now facing about and forgetting all her anger in hearing what Anna had to tell. So Anna went on and described all that had happened, imitating London's cry of terror at the sight of the "white witches." At this Luretta began to laugh, and Anna came nearer to the big chair, and even ventured to rest against its arm.

"Luretta, let's you and I go up the trail toward the forest. Perhaps we might find Trit and Trot," she suggested.

Luretta was out of the chair in a moment; and, quite forgetting all her anger toward Anna, she agreed promptly and the two little girls, hand in hand, came into the kitchen and told Mrs. Foster their plan.

She listened smilingly, but cautioned them not to go beyond the edge of the forest.

"You might meet some animal larger than a rabbit," she warned them; " 'tis the time when bears are about nibbling the tender bark and buds of the young trees; so go not into the wood. Beside that a party of Indians were seen near the upper falls yesterday."

"But the Indians come often to the village, and do no harm," said Anna.

But Mrs. Foster shook her head. She remembered that the Indians could not always be trusted. The little girls promised to follow the trail only to the edge of the wood, and started soberly off.

"We might see Trit and Trot behind any bush, might we not?" suggested Luretta hopefully.

"Perhaps we might see a little baby bear! Would it not be fine if we could catch two little bears instead of rabbits?" responded Anna, as they climbed the hill, stopping now and then to pick the tender young checkerberry leaves, or listen to the song of some woodland bird. A group of young spruce trees stood beside the trail, and here the two little girls stopped to rest. The sun was warm, and they both were glad to sit down in the pleasant shade.

They talked about the *Polly*, wondering when she would come to port, and then their thoughts went back to their lost pets.

"I do think you ought not to have taken them from the box. I am sure Paul will not like it when I tell him they are gone," said Luretta.

Anna's face grew grave. "Must you tell him?" she asked.

"Of course I must. He will bring home young leaves and roots for them to-night, and what will he say!" and Luretta's voice sounded as if tears were very near.

While Luretta spoke Anna's eyes had been fixed on a little clump of bushes on the other side of the trail. The bushes moved queerly. There was no wind, and Anna was sure that some little animal was hiding behind the shrubs. Greatly excited, Anna leaned forward, grasping Luretta's arm.

"Look! those bushes!" she whispered.

At that moment a queer ball of dingy white appeared on the opposite side of the trail, and instantly Anna sprang toward it. Her hands grasped the torn and twisted piece of floating cloth, and closed upon the poor frightened little creature, one of the lost rabbits, nearly frightened to death by the strange garment that had prevented his escape.

If he could have spoken he would have begged for the freedom that his brother had achieved; but he could only tremble and shrink from the tender hands that held him so firmly.

In a moment Anna had unfastened the doll's skirt, and Trit, or Trot, was once more clear of the detested garment.

"Oh, Danna! Do you suppose we can take it safely home?" exclaimed the delighted Luretta.

"Just see how frightened he is," Anna responded. Somehow she no longer wished to take the little creature back and shut it up.

"Do you suppose its mother is trying to find it?" she continued thoughtfully.

"And would it tell its brothers and sisters all its adventures, just as Mother said?" questioned Luretta.

"Why not?" Anna's brown eyes sparkled. "Of course it would. Probably Trot is safe home by this time, and all the rabbit family are looking out for Trit."

Anna looked hopefully toward Luretta. If Trit went free it must be Luretta's gift. Anna felt that she had no right to decide.

"Let him go, Danna," said Luretta softly; and very gently Anna released her clasp on the soft little rabbit. It looked quickly up, and with a bound it was across the trail and out of sight.

Both the girls drew a long breath.

"I will tell Paul about Trit's mother and brothers and sisters," said Luretta, as they started toward home. "Probably he will laugh; but I guess he will say they ought to be free."

Both Anna and Luretta were very quiet on the walk home. Anna began to feel tired. It seemed to her that a great deal had happened since morning. She remembered the liberty pole, with a little guilty sense of having been more interested in the rabbits, and in Melvina and Luretta, than in the safety of the emblem of freedom. But she was glad that Luretta was no longer angry at her.

"You don't care much about the rabbits, do you, Danna?" Luretta asked, as they stopped near Luretta's house to say good-bye.

"I am glad they are free," replied Anna. "It would be dreadful to have giants catch us, wouldn't it?"

Luretta agreed soberly, thinking that to the rabbits she must have seemed a giant.

"Father will say 'twas best to let them go, whatever Paul says," she added, and promising to meet the next day the friends parted.

Anna danced along the path in her old fashion, quite forgetting Melvina's measured steps. Everything was all right now. She and Luretta were friends; Mrs. Foster had pardoned her; and the liberty pole was found. So she was smiling and happy as she pushed open the door and entered the pleasant kitchen, expecting to see her mother and Rebby; but no one was there. The room looked deserted. She opened the door leading into the front room and her happy smile vanished.

Her mother sat there, looking very grave and anxious; and facing the kitchen door and looking straight at Anna was Mrs. Lyon, while on a stool beside her sat Melvina, her flounced linen skirt and embroidered white sunbonnet as white as a gull's breast.

Anna looked from one to the other wonderingly. Of course, she thought, Mrs. Lyon had come to call her a mischievous girl on account of the rabbits. All her happiness vanished; and when her mother said: "Come in, Anna. Mrs. Lyon has come on purpose to speak with you," she quite forgot to curtsy to the minister's wife, and stood silent and afraid.

CHAPTER XI

AN EXCHANGE OF VISITS

"IT is Mr. Lyon's suggestion," concluded Mrs. Lyon, "and Melvina is eager to come and live with you, Mrs. Weston, if Anna is ready to come to me."

Mrs. Lyon, it seemed to Anna, had been talking a long time. She had said that Melvina was not very strong, and that possibly she was kept too much indoors; and then had come the astounding suggestion that, on the very next day, Anna should go and live with the minister and his wife, and Melvina should come and take her place.

"Oh, do, Anna! Say you will," Melvina whispered, as the two little girls found a chance to speak together while their mothers discussed the plan. For Melvina was sure that if she came to live in Anna's home she would become exactly like Anna; as brave and as independent, and who could tell but what she might grow to look like her as well!

The same thought came to Anna. Of course, if she lived with Mrs. Lyon she would learn to behave exactly like Melvina. But to go away from her father and mother and from Rebby; this seemed hardly to be possible.

"Do you want me to go, Mother?" she asked, half hoping that her mother might say at once that it was not to be thought of.

"I must talk with your father; 'tis a great opportunity for your good, and I am sure he will be pleased," replied Mrs. Weston. For had not the Reverend Mr. Lyon written a book, and, it was rumored, composed music for hymns; for any little girl to live in his family would be a high privilege. And this was what Mr. Weston thought when he heard of the plan.

"Why, it is a wise scheme indeed," he said gravely; "my little Danna is being too much favored at home, and to be with the minister and his wife will teach her as much as a term in school."

"But I am not to stay long, Father. I am only to stay for two weeks," said Anna, "and you must not learn to think Melvina is your little girl."

"Mr. Lyon wishes Melvina to run about as freely as we have allowed Anna," Mrs. Weston explained, "and to have no lessons or tasks of any kind, and to spend an hour each afternoon at home while Anna does the same."

"But I am to have lessons, just as if I were Melvina," Anna declared, and before bedtime it was decided that on the next day Anna should go to the minister's to remain a fortnight.

Rebecca was the only one who did not think well of the plan. "I do not want Danna to go," she said over and over; and added that she should not know how to treat Melvina, or what to say to her. It was Rebecca who went with Anna to Mr. Lyon, carrying the small package containing Anna's clothing, and she brought back Melvina's carefully packed basket. Mrs. Lyon looked worried and anxious as she saw Melvina start off for the Westons'; but she gave her no cautions or directions, beyond telling her to be obedient to Mrs. Weston. Then she took Anna's hand and led her up-stairs to the pleasant room where she and Melvina had played so happily with the rabbits.

"You can leave your sunbonnet here, Anna, and then come down to the library. This is the hour for your lesson in English history."

" 'English history,' " Anna repeated to herself excitedly. She wondered what it could mean. But if it was something that Melvina did she was eager to begin.

Mr. Lyon smiled down at his little visitor as she curtsied in the doorway. He hoped his own little daughter might return with eyes as bright and cheeks as glowing.

"This is where Melvina sits for her study hour," he said, pointing to a small chair near a side window. There was a table in front of the chair, and on the table was spread a brightly colored map.

"To-day we are to discover something of the English opinion of Americans," began Mr. Lyon, taking up a small book. "It is always wise to know the important affairs of the time in which we live, is it not, Anna?" he said thoughtfully.

"Yes, sir," responded Anna seriously, sitting very straight indeed and feeling of greater consequence than ever before.

"America's great trouble now, remember, is taxation without representation," continued the minister; "and now listen carefully to what an Englishman has to say of it: 'While England contends for the right of taxing America we are giving up substance for the shadow; we are exchanging happiness for pride. If we have no regard for America, let us at least respect the mother country. In a dispute with America who would we conquer? Ourselves. Everything that injures America is injurious to Great Britain, and we commit a kind of political suicide when we endeavor to crush them into obedience.'

"Ah! There is still wisdom in the English council; but I fear it is too late," said Mr. Lyon, as if speaking his thoughts aloud. "And now, my child, what is the subject of our lesson?" he questioned, looking kindly at Anna.

"England and America," she replied promptly.

Mr. Lyon nodded. "And why does America firmly resolve not to be unjustly taxed?" he asked.

"Because it wouldn't be right," said Anna confidently.

Mr. Lyon was evidently pleased by her direct answers.

"If an Englishman sees the injustice of his government it is small wonder that every American, even to a little girl, can see that it is not to be borne," said Mr. Lyon, rising and pacing up and down the narrow room, his thoughts full of the great conflict that had already begun between England and her American colonies.

Anna's eyes turned toward the map. There was a long yellow strip marked "American Colonies," then, lower down, a number of red blots and circles with "The West Indies" printed across them. Far over on the end of the map was a queerly shaped green object marked "Asia" and below it a beautiful blue place called "Europe." Anna was so delighted and interested in discovering France, and Africa, the Aegean Sea, and the British Isles, that she quite forgot where she was. But as she looked at the very small enclosure marked "England," and then at the long line of America she suddenly exclaimed: "America need not be afraid."

Mr. Lyon had seated himself at his desk, and at the sound of Anna's voice he looked up in surprise.

"Why, child! You have been so quiet I had forgotten you. Run out to the sitting-room to Mrs. Lyon," and Anna obeyed, not forgetting to curtsy as she left the room.

Mrs. Lyon had a basket piled high with work. There were stockings to be darned, pillow-cases to be neatly repaired, and an apron of stout drilling to be hemmed. Anna's task was to darn stockings. She was given Melvina's thimble to use, a smooth wooden ball to slip into the stocking, and a needle and skein of cotton.

How long the afternoon seemed! Never before had Anna stayed indoors for the whole of a May afternoon. She felt tired and sleepy, and did not want to walk about the garden after supper—as Mrs. Lyon kindly suggested; and not until Mrs. Lyon said that Melvina, on every pleasant day, walked about the garden after supper, did Anna go slowly down the path. But she stood at the gate looking in the direction of her home with wistful eyes.

"Two weeks," she whispered; it seemed so long a time could never pass. Then she remembered that the next day she would go home for the daily visit agreed upon.

If the days passed slowly with Anna, to Melvina they seemed only too short. She had quickly made friends with Rebecca, and the elder girl was astonished at the daring spirit of the minister's daughter. Melvina would balance herself on the very edge of the bluff, when she and Rebby, often followed by a surprised and unhappy Luretta, went for a morning walk. Or on their trips to the lumber yard for chips Melvina would climb to the top of some pile of timber and dance about as if trying to make Rebby

HOW LONG THE AFTERNOON SEEMED!

frightened lest she fall. She went wading along the shore, and brought home queerly shaped rocks and tiny mussel-shells; and, as her father had hoped, her cheeks grew rosy and her eyes bright.

The day set for the erection of the liberty pole was the last day of the "exchange visit" of the two little girls; and Anna was now sure that Mrs. Lyon must think her very much like Melvina, for she had learned her daily lessons obediently, and moved about the house as quietly as a mouse.

But when she awoke on the morning of the day upon which she was to return home she was sure it was the happiest day of her life. Mrs. Lyon had even called her a "quiet and careful child," and the minister smiled upon her, and said that she "was a loyal little maid." So she had great reason for being pleased; and the thought of being home again made her ready to dance with delight.

The day that the tree of liberty was planted was declared a holiday, and the inhabitants of the town gathered on the bluff where it was to be set. Melvina and Anna and Luretta were together, and the other children of the neighborhood were scattered about.

"Where is Rebby, Mother?" Anna asked, looking about for her sister. "

"To be sure! She started off with Lucia Horton, but I do not see them," responded Mrs. Weston, smiling happily to think that her own little Danna would no longer be absent from home.

There was great rejoicing among the people as the tree was raised, and citizen after citizen stepped forward and made solemn pledges to resist England's injustice to the American colonies. Then, amid the shouts of the assembled inhabitants, the discharge of musketry, and the sound of fife and drum, Machias took its rightful place among the defenders of American liberty.

But Rebecca Weston and Lucia Horton, sitting in an upper window of the Horton house, looked out at the inspiring scene without wishing to be any nearer. Rebecca was ashamed when she remembered her own part in trying to prevent the erection of a liberty pole, for now she realized all it stood for; and she was no longer afraid of an attack upon the town by an English gunboat. To Rebecca it seemed that such an attack would bring its own punishment. Her thoughts were now filled by a great desire to do something, something difficult and even dangerous to her own safety, in order to make up for that evening when she had crept out in the darkness and helped Lucia send the tree adrift.

But Lucia's mind was filled with entirely different thoughts. She was ready to cry with disappointment and fear in seeing the liberty pole set up. She could not forget that her father had said that such a thing would mean trouble.

"If we had not set it adrift, Lucia, we could be on the bluff now with the others," Rebby whispered, as they heard the gay notes of the fife.

"Bosh! Who wants to be any nearer? My mother says 'tis a silly and foolish performance," replied Lucia. "But perhaps 'twill be cut down before the *Polly* comes into harbor."

Rebecca jumped up from the window-seat, her face flushed and her eyes shining.

"No one would dare, Lucia Horton. And if it is cut down I'll know you, or someone in this house, planned it; and I will tell my father just what you told me and what we did," she exclaimed, starting toward the door.

"You can't tell, ever, Rebecca Weston! You promised not to," Lucia called after her, and Rebecca stopped suddenly. Lucia was right. No matter what happened she could never reveal what Lucia had told her, because of her promise; and a promise was a sacred thing.

Without a word of good-bye Rebecca went slowly down the stairs. This was the second time she had left the Horton house in anger. "I won't come here again," she thought, a little sadly, for she and Lucia had been "best friends" ever since Captain Horton had brought his family to the remote settlement.

"There's Rebby," Anna called joyfully, as holding her father's hand, and with her mother walking close behind, she came along the path toward home. Rebby was walking slowly along a short distance in front of the little party, and Anna soon overtook her.

"Oh, Rebby! Was it not a splendid sight to see the liberty tree set up?" Anna exclaimed eagerly, "and all the men taking off their hats and cheering?"

"Yes," responded Rebby briefly; and then looking at Anna she said: "Oh, Danna! I wish, more than anything, that I could do something to protect the liberty tree."

"Perhaps you can, Rebby, sometime, you and I together," replied Anna hopefully; "anyway, isn't it lovely that I am home to stay?"

And to this Rebby could agree smilingly, but she kept in her heart the wish she had just uttered.

CHAPTER XII

WILD HONEY

ANNA went singing about the house quite satisfied now to be herself; and Rebby and her mother smiled at each other at the happiness of the little girl.

"I doubt not you have learned many things, Danna," said Rebby, a little wistfully, as the sisters sat on the broad door-step after supper looking down at the broad flowing river.

"Yes, indeed!" replied Anna confidently. "Why, Rebby, I know all about history. The minister told me that a hundred and fifty years ago there were English traders living right here, and they were driven away by the French. And then, some forty years ago, Governor Belcher of Massachusetts came cruising along this coast, and there was no one at all here. And, Rebby, Mr. Lyon says there are no such pine forests in all the colonies as stretch along behind this settlement. But, Rebby, you are not listening!" and Anna looked reproachfully at her sister.

"Oh, yes, indeed, Danna, I heard every word. And I heard Father say that very soon there would be a regular school here, with a master, as soon as

America conquers her enemies. But, Danna, do you suppose anyone will dare touch the liberty pole?" For Rebby's thoughts could not long stray from Lucia Horton's prediction that it might be cut down.

"What's that?" exclaimed Mr. Weston from the doorway behind them.

"Cut down the liberty pole? Why, there is not a man in Machias who would do such a traitorous deed."

Rebby's face flushed scarlet at his words, but before she could speak, her father continued: "Well, Danna, are you ready for a day's tramp with me to-morrow? I must go up to the mill at Kwapskitchwock Falls, and we will start early."

"Oh, yes!" exclaimed Danna, jumping up and clasping her father's hand. "And perhaps we shall catch a salmon above the falls, and broil it over a fire for our dinner."

"That is what we will hope to do," replied Mr. Weston. "And, Rebby, why do you not come with us? 'Tis but a few miles, and a day in the woods will do you good."

"Why, perhaps I shall, if Mother does not need me," Rebby answered. She so seldom cared for woodland tramps that Anna gave a little exclamation of surprised delight.

"I'll make a corn-cake to take with us," Rebby added, "and since we start early I had best bake it to-night," and she went into the kitchen followed by Anna singing:

> "We'll go to the forest of liberty trees,
> Where there are rabbits and birds and bees."

Mrs. Weston smiled as she listened. "'Twould indeed be fine if you could find a store of wild honey in the woods; 'twould be a great help," she said, measuring out the golden meal for Rebby to use for her corn-cake. There was no butter or eggs to use in its making, for all food was getting scarce in most of the loyal households. Rebby scalded the meal and stirred it carefully, then added milk, and turned the batter into an iron pan which she set over the fire. When it was cooked it would be a thin crispy cake that would be appetizing and nourishing. Rebby's thoughts traveled away to the dainties of the Hortons' cupboard, but she said to herself that the "spider cake," as the corn-cake was called, especially when eaten in the woods with freshly broiled salmon, would taste far better than the jellies and preserved fruits of the Hortons. Rebby could not forget Mrs. Horton's scorn of the liberty pole.

The Westons were up at an early hour the next morning. The sun was just showing itself above the tops of the tall pines when the family sat down to their simple breakfast. Anna wore her skirt of tanned deerskin, moccasins, and her blouse of home-made flannel, while Rebecca's dress was of stout cotton. Each of the girls wore round, turban-like hats. Anna's was trimmed with the scarlet wings of a red bird, while Rebby's had the white breast of a gull.

Mr. Weston wore deerskin breeches and moccasins and a flannel blouse. A stout leather belt about his waist carried a couple of serviceable knives, and he carried his musket, for the forest was filled with many wild animals, and the settlers were always ready to protect themselves.

Rebby carried a basket that held the corn-cake, and a flint and steel from which they would strike the spark for their noonday fire.

Anna ran along close beside her father, until the path narrowed so that only one could walk, followed by the others. The air was cool and full of the forest odors. Now and then birds flitted past them, and once or twice Anna had a glimpse of startled rabbits, which she was sure were Trit and Trot.

"If I could only catch one to give Luretta," she thought, "then she would forgive me for taking the other rabbits," for Anna's thoughts were often troubled because of the loss of Luretta's pets.

Mr. Weston stopped at one point to show his daughters an arrow marked on a tall pine and pointing east. "That is to show the beginning of the path to

Chandler's River settlement," he explained. "The trail is so dim that the woodsmen have blazed the trees to show the way. There is a good store of powder and shot at Chandler's River," he added, a little thoughtfully.

Rebby looked at the arrow, and afterward she had reason to remember her father's words.

The mill at Kwapskitchwock Falls was not in use at the time of their visit, and the mill workers were in Machias. But great booms of logs, waiting to be sawed into lumber, lay all along the river banks.

The sun was high in the heavens when the little party came in sight of the falls dashing over the rocks.

Mr. Weston led the way to a big flat rock above the mill, and where two large beech trees cast a pleasant shade.

"You can rest here while I look over the mill," he said, "and then I will see if I can spear a salmon for our dinner."

The girls were quite ready to rest, and Rebby set the basket carefully on the rock beside them.

"Would it not be fine if we could catch a salmon and have it all cooked when Father comes back?" Anna suggested, but Rebby shook her head.

"We haven't any salmon spear, and it is quick and skilful work," she responded. "Father will be better pleased if we obey him and rest here."

From where the girls were sitting they could look some distance up the quiet stream, and it was Anna who first discovered a canoe being paddled close to the opposite shore.

"Look, Rebby," she said, pointing in the direction of the slow-moving craft. "Isn't that an Indian?"

Rebby looked, and after a moment answered: "Why, I suppose it is, and after salmon. But he won't come down so near the falls." But the girls watched the slow-moving canoe rather anxiously until it drew close in to the opposite shore, and was hidden by the overhanging branches of the trees.

Rebby decided that she would gather some dry grass and sticks for the fire, and asked Anna to go down near the mill and bring up some of the bits of wood lying about there.

"Then when Father does bring the salmon we can start a blaze right away," she said.

Anna ran off toward the mill yard, and Rebby left the shade of the big beeches to pull handfuls of the sun-dried grass.

Rebby had gone but a few steps when she heard a queer singing murmur that seemed to be just above her head. She looked up, but the sky was clear; there was no bird flying low, as she had imagined; but as she walked along the murmur became louder, and Rebby began to look about her more carefully. A short distance from the flat rock was a huge stump of a broken tree, and Rebby soon realized that the noise came from the stump, and she approached it cautiously.

"Oh!" she exclaimed. "It's a honey-tree! It is! It is!" for she had seen the bees as they went steadily in a dark murmuring line, direct to the old stump.

"A honey-tree" was a fortunate discovery at any time, for it meant a store of delicious wild honey. It was, as in this case, usually a partially decayed tree where the wild bees had swarmed, and where stores of honey were concealed. Sometimes the bees had filled the cavities of the tree so full that they were forced to desert it and find new quarters; but it was evident that here they were very busy indeed.

"They will have to be smoked out," decided Rebby, who had often heard her father tell of the way in which such stores were captured. "I wish I could do it, and get some honey for dinner," she exclaimed aloud.

"Well, why not?" she heard someone say from behind her, and she turned quickly to find Paul Foster, looking so much like an Indian boy in his fringed leggins and feathered cap that it made her jump quickly.

Paul laughed at her surprise.

"I came up-stream in my canoe after salmon," he explained, "and I have speared three beauties; I saw you from across the stream, so I paddled over. You've made a great find," and he nodded toward the old stump.

"Could we smoke out the bees and get some honey, Paul?" Rebby asked eagerly. She and Paul were nearly of an age, and Paul was a friendly boy, always ready to make bows and arrows or toy boats for his little sister and her girl playmates.

"I don't see why not," he responded, as if smoking out a hive of wild bees was a very usual undertaking; "but I haven't a flint and steel," he added.

"I have, in my basket," declared Rebecca; and in a few minutes Paul and Rebecca had gathered a mass of sticks and grass, heaping it a short distance from the stump.

"Mustn't get a blaze, only a heavy smoke," said Paul as he struck the flint and steel together, and carefully sheltered the spark which the dry grass instantly caught.

At the sight of the smoke Mr. Weston came running from the mill, and with his assistance the bees were speedily disposed of.

The old stump proved well filled with honey.

"I have a bucket in my canoe," said Paul, and it was decided to fill the bucket and take home all it would hold, and to return the next day in Paul's canoe with tubs for the rest of the honey.

Paul insisted that Mr. Weston should accept one of his fine salmon to broil for their midday meal, and then Rebby exclaimed:

"Where is Danna? She went to the mill after wood before we found the honey-tree, and she isn't back yet."

"Oh! She is probably playing that she is an explorer on a journey to the South Seas," laughed Mr. Weston. "I will go after her," and he started off toward the mill, while Rebecca added wood to the fire, and Paul prepared the salmon to broil.

Mr. Weston called "Danna!" repeatedly, but there was no answer. He searched the yard and the shore, but there was no trace of his little daughter. He went through the big open mill, and peered into shadowy corners, but Anna was not to be found. And at last he hurried back to tell Paul and Rebby, and to have them help him in his search for the missing girl.

CHAPTER XIII

DOWN THE RIVER

ANNA had gathered an armful of dry wood and was just starting back when a queer little frightened cry made her stop suddenly and look quickly around. In a moment the noise was repeated, and she realized that it came from a pile of logs near the river bank. Anna put down the wood, and tiptoed carefully in the direction of the sound.

As she came near the logs she could see a little gray creature struggling to get loose from a coil of string in which its hind legs were entangled.

"Oh! It's a rabbit!" Anna exclaimed. "Perhaps it is Trit," and she ran quickly forward. But the little creature was evidently more alarmed at her approach than at the trap that held him, and with a frantic leap he was off, the string trailing behind him; but his hind feet were still hampered by the twisting string, and he came to a sudden halt.

"Poor Trit! Poor Trit!" called the little girl pityingly, as she ran after him. Just as she was near enough to touch him another bound carried him beyond her reach. On leaped the rabbit, and on followed Anna until they were some distance below the mill and near the river's sloping bank, over which the rabbit plunged and Anna after him. A small boat lay close to the shore, and Bunny's plunge carried him directly into the boat, where, twisted in the string, he lay struggling and helpless.

Anna climbed into the boat and picked up "Trit," as she called the rabbit, and patiently and tenderly untied the string from the frightened, panting little captive, talking gently as she did so, until he lay quiet in her hands.

The little girl was so wholly absorbed in her task that she did not notice that the boat was not fastened, or that her spring into it had sent it clear from the shore. Not until Trit was free from the string did she look up, and then the little boat was several feet from the shore, and moving rapidly down-stream.

If Anna had stepped overboard then she could easily have waded ashore and made her way back to the mill; but she was so surprised that such a course did not come into her thoughts, and in a few moments the boat was in deep water and moving with the current down-stream.

On each side of the river the woods grew down to the shore, and now and then the wide branches of overhanging trees stretched for some distance over the stream. A blue heron rose from the river, making its loud call that drowned Anna's voice as she cried: "Father! Father!" Even had Mr. Weston been near at hand he could hardly have distinguished Anna's voice. But Anna was now too far down-stream for any call to reach her father or Rebby and Paul, who were all anxiously searching for her.

At first the little girl was not at all frightened. The river ran to Machias, and, had it not been that she was sure her father and sister would be worried and sadly troubled by her disappearance, Anna would have thought it a fine adventure to go sailing down the stream with her captured rabbit. Even as it was, she had a gleeful thought of Luretta's surprise and of Melvina's admiration when she should tell them the story.

She soon discovered that the boat leaked, and, holding the rabbit tightly in one hand, she took off her round cap and began to bail out the water, which had now risen to her ankles. Very soon the little cap was soggy and dripping; and now Anna began to wonder how long the leaky little craft could keep afloat.

Both Anna and Rebby could swim; their father had taught them when they were very little girls, and Anna knew that if she would leave the rabbit to drown that she could reach the shore safely; but this seemed hardly to be thought of. She now resolved to clutch at the first branch within reach, hoping in that way to scramble to safety with Trit. But the boat was being carried steadily along by the current, although the water came in constantly about her feet.

"I mustn't get frightened," Anna said aloud, remembering how often her father had told her that to be afraid was to lose the battle.

The boat swayed a little, and then Anna found that the board seat was wabbling.

"I never thought of the seat," she whispered, slipping down to her knees and pulling the seat from the loose support on which it rested. It was hard work to use the board as a paddle with only one hand, but Anna was strong and resolute, and managed to swing the boat a little toward the shore, so when a turn of the river came, bringing the boat close toward a little point of land, she quickly realized that this was her opportunity, and holding Trit close she sprang into the shallow water and in a moment was safe on shore.

The old boat, now half-filled with water, moved slowly on, and Anna knew that it would not be long afloat. She looked about her landing-place with wondering eyes. Behind the little grassy point where she stood the forest stretched close and dark; the curve of the river shut away the course by which she had come, but she could look down the smooth flowing current, and toward the wooded shores opposite.

The rabbit moved uneasily in her hands, and the little girl smoothed him tenderly. "I don't know who will ever find me here, unless it should be Indians," she said aloud, remembering the canoe that she and Rebby had noticed as they sat on the big rock.

Anna felt a little choking feeling in her throat at the remembrance. It seemed so long ago since she had seen Rebby and her father. "And it's all your fault, Trit," she told the rabbit; "but you could not help it," she added quickly, and remembered that the rabbit must be hungry and thirsty, and for a little while busied herself in finding tender leaves and buds for Trit to eat, and in holding him close to the water's edge so that he could drink. Then she wandered about the little clearing and to the edge of the dark forest. She began to feel hungry, and knew by the sun that it was well past noon.

"Oh! If that Indian we saw in the canoe would only come down-stream," she thought longingly. For Anna well knew that when night came she would be in danger from the wild beasts of the wilderness, but that almost any of the Indians who fished and hunted in that region would take her safely back to her home.

An hour or two dragged slowly by; Anna was very tired. She held Trit close, and sat down not far from the river's edge. "Father will find me some way," she said to herself over and over, and tried not to let thoughts of fear and loneliness find a place in her mind. The little wild rabbit was no longer afraid of its captor, and Anna was sure that it was sorry it had led her into such trouble. But now and then tears came to the little girl's eyes, when suddenly she heard a voice from the river just above the curve singing a familiar air:

"Success to fair America,—
To courage to be free,
Success to fair America,
Success to Liberty."

"Oh! That is Paul! That is Paul!" cried Anna, jumping up and down with joy; and the next moment a canoe swung round the curve, paddled by a tall boy with a cap ornamented by tall feathers.

Paul nearly dropped his paddle as he saw Anna at the river's edge.

"However did you get here?" he exclaimed, as with a swift stroke of his paddle he sent his canoe to shore.

Anna told him quickly of the capture of Trit, the leaking boat, and her jump to safety, while Paul listened with astonished eyes, and, in his turn, told of the discovery of the honey-tree, and then of the search for Anna.

"Your father and Rebby are sadly frightened," he concluded; "they are well on the way home now, thinking possibly you might have followed the path. Now, get in the canoe, and I'll try my best to get you home by the time they reach the settlement."

Anna sat in the bottom of the canoe, and Paul skilfully wielded the paddle, sending the little craft swiftly down the river.

"That bucket is full of honey," he said, nodding toward the bow of the canoe. But Anna was not greatly interested in the honey; she had even forgotten that she was hungry and thirsty. She could think only of her father and Rebby searching along the path for some trace of her.

It was late in the afternoon when the canoe swept across the river to the same landing where Paul had fastened the liberty tree earlier in the month. And in a few moments Anna was running up the path toward home, followed by Paul with the bucket of honey.

"Why, child! Where are Father and Rebby? and where is your cap?" questioned Mrs. Weston.

"Oh, Mother!" began Anna, but now the tears could not be kept back, and held close in her mother's arms she sobbed out the story of the capture of Trit, and all that had followed. And then Paul told the story of the honey-tree, and his story was not finished when Anna exclaimed: "Father! Rebby!" and ran toward the door.

How Mr. Weston's face brightened when he saw Danna safe and sound, and how closely Rebby held her little sister, as Anna again told the story of her journey down the river.

When Paul started for home Mrs. Weston insisted that a generous portion of the bucket of honey should go with him; and Trit, safely fastened in a small basket, was sent to Luretta as a gift from Anna. He promised to be ready the next morning to return to the falls with Mr. Weston in the canoe to bring home the store of honey.

As the Westons gathered about the table for their evening meal they looked at each other with happy faces.

"I couldn't feel happier if the *Polly* were in port, and America triumphant over her enemies," declared Mr. Weston, as he helped Anna to a liberal portion of honey.

CHAPTER XIV

AN UNINVITED GUEST

PAUL and Mr. Weston started off at an early hour the next morning in Paul's canoe to bring home the honey. Beside a tub they took with them a number of buckets, for the old stump had a rich store of honey.

It was a time of leisure for the lumbering settlement. The drives of logs had all come down the river and were safely in the booms. The mills could not run as usual, for the conflict with England made it difficult to send lumber to Boston. The crops were now planted, so Mr. Weston, like other men of the settlement, had time for hunting and fishing or for improving their simple homes. Some of the men passed a good part of each day lounging around the shores and wharves, looking anxiously down the harbor hoping to see Captain Jones' sloops returning with the greatly needed provisions.

Rebecca was up in season to see her father start, but Anna, tired from the adventure of the previous day, had not awakened.

"Is the liberty tree safe?" Rebby asked a little anxiously, as she helped her mother about the household work that morning.

"Why, Rebby dear, what harm could befall it?" questioned her mother. "The traitor who set it afloat will not dare cut it down. 'Tis a strange thing that, search though they may, no trace can be found of the rascals."

Rebecca's hands trembled, and she dared not look up. It seemed to the little girl that if her mother should look into her eyes she would at once know that she, Rebecca Flora Weston, who had been born in Boston, and whose parents were loyal Americans, had committed the dreadful deed. She wished with all her heart that she could tell her mother all that Lucia Horton had said; but the promise bound her. She could never tell anyone. Rebecca knew that she could never be happy again. "Not unless I could do some fine thing to help America," she thought, a little hopelessly; for what could a little girl, in a settlement far away from all the strife, do to help the great cause for which unselfish men were sacrificing everything?

Mrs. Weston was troubled about Rebecca. "The child has not really been well since her birthday," she thought, "although I cannot think what the trouble can be."

"Your father says that the honey is really yours, Rebby dear," continued Mrs. Weston, "and that you may decide how it shall be disposed of."

"I don't care," Rebby responded, a little faintly. "Only, of course, Paul ought to have half, because he helped."

"Yes, of course; but even then your share will be a good quantity," said Mrs. Weston. Before Rebecca could speak Anna came running into the room, her brown eyes shining, and her curls, now long enough to dance about her face, falling over her brown cheeks.

As she ate her porridge her mother questioned her about the adventure of the previous day, and for a time Rebby forgot her own worries in listening to Anna's account of her journey in the leaking boat, and of her leap to safety.

"It was not mischief, was it, Mother, to try and capture Trit?" she concluded.

"No, indeed, dear child. Who could foresee such an adventure?" replied Mrs. Weston. "And we are all proud that you did so well; that you did not wander into the forest, where you would surely have been lost. I was just asking Rebby what use we would make of the honey. Of course we want to share it with our neighbors. 'Tis rare good fortune to have such a store of sweets."

"Let's have a honey party," suggested Anna. "Could we not, Mother?"

"Why, that is a splendid idea!" declared Mrs. Weston. " 'Twill cheer up the whole settlement to be asked to a party. To be sure I can offer them only honey; but perhaps 'twill take their minds from the *Polly*, and from England's injustice toward us. Rebecca, you and Anna shall start out at once and ask the neighbors as far as Mr. Lyon's house. That will bring as many as twenty people. And tell each one to bring a cup and spoon, as I have no extra dishes."

As soon as Anna had finished her breakfast the two girls put on their sunbonnets and started on their pleasant errand. The neighbors were to be asked to come the next afternoon for a taste of wild honey, and Mrs. Weston again cautioned them to be sure and speak of the cup and spoon that each guest was to bring.

"I wish I could offer them a dish of tea," thought Mrs. Weston, and then reproached herself for the thought, for was not the tea tax one of England's sins against the colonies, and had not loyal women refused to brew a single cup until America gained her rights?

Mr. Foster was busy in his blacksmith shop. The mill men could be idle, but Worden Foster hammered busily away day in and day out. His hay-forks were always in demand, and he made many stout locks and keys, as well as door-latches and hooks.

"Shall we ask him first?" questioned Anna.

"Yes," replied Rebecca. "He is our best neighbor, so 'tis right to ask him first."

Rebecca and Anna stood in the open doorway for a moment watching the glow of the forge and the bright sparks that sprang from the red bar of iron which Mr. Foster was shaping into a spearhead.

He nodded toward his little visitors smilingly, and listened with evident pleasure to Rebecca's invitation.

"But you tell me Paul is to have a good portion of the honey; 'tis hardly fair we Fosters should come," he replied, and then added quickly, "But why not let us have the neighbors, and divide the honey that is left after the party?"

"Why, yes, sir; I think that will be a good plan," responded Rebby soberly, "and perhaps Luretta will go with us to ask the neighbors."

Mr. Foster nodded again, whistling softly to himself, and as the little girls bade him a polite "Good-morning" and went on toward his house they could hear his whistle ring above the sound of his hammer.

Luretta came running to meet them.

"I was just coming to your house to thank you for Trit. Oh, Anna! You are the bravest girl in the settlement. Paul says you are. And to think you caught the rabbit for me." Luretta, quite out of breath, with her arm across Anna's shoulders, looked admiringly at her friend.

"It's only fair," Anna replied, "because I lost yours." And then Anna had to tell again the story of her capture of Trit. Luretta listened eagerly. "I do wish I could have been with you, Danna," she said. But Anna shook her head. "The boat would have sunk," she responded soberly.

Mrs. Foster thought the plan for a honey party an excellent idea, and promised to come in good season; and Luretta was greatly pleased to go with her friends to invite the neighbors.

"Will not Lucia Horton be pleased when we tell her about the honey?" said Anna.

Rebecca stopped suddenly. "We are not to ask the Hortons," she announced.

"Not ask Lucia! Why not?" questioned Anna, while Luretta looked at Rebby with wondering eyes.

"No," Rebecca declared firmly. "The Hortons have a cupboard filled with jellies, and candied fruits, and jars of syrups, and fine things from the West Indies and from far places, and 'tis not fair. We have only the wild bees' honey, a taste for each neighbor." Rebecca stopped with a little sigh. She had not thought about not asking Lucia until Anna spoke, but now she realized that, if she could help it, she would never again go to the Hortons' house. Rebecca was old enough to realize the difference between loyalty and selfish indecision, and she was sure that the Hortons were thinking more of their own comfort than of the good of America.

"But Lucia is your best friend," said Anna; "she gave you those beautiful silk mitts on your birthday."

Rebecca's face colored. She made no answer. The silk mitts, she resolved, must be given back. Probably she would never have another pair; but never mind, if she gave up Lucia's friendship she must give up the mitts.

For a few minutes the little girls walked on in silence, but Luretta was eager to talk about Trit, and very soon she and Anna were talking happily of plans to teach the captured rabbit, and were no longer troubled by Rebecca's decision not to ask the Hortons to the honey party. If they thought of it at all it was to agree with Rebby: that people with a cupboard full of dainties, when their neighbors had only the coarsest fare, ought not to be asked to share the wild honey.

Mrs. Lyon welcomed the little girls in a most friendly manner, and Anna was made happy when the minister's wife said that she really believed that Anna's stitches were as tiny and as neatly set as those of Melvina herself.

"Melvina is out-of-doors," she continued; "I have decided that she is much stronger to be in the open air a portion of each day, and London has made her a playhouse under the pines behind the house."

Both Anna and Luretta hoped that Mrs. Lyon would ask them to go and see Melvina's playhouse, but as she did not they said their polite "Good-day, Mrs. Lyon," curtsied, and followed Rebecca down the path.

The invitations had now all been given and accepted, and Luretta was eager to get home, urging Anna to stop and see Trit, who was safe in the same box that had been made for the other rabbits.

"You may both run ahead if you wish," said Rebby with quite a grown-up manner, for she really felt a great deal older than her little sister, "and I will go straight home and tell Mother that everybody is coming."

"Everybody except the Hortons," Luretta reminded her.

"Yes; I meant everyone whom we had asked," Rebby rejoined.

Off ran the two younger girls, and Rebecca followed more slowly. Although she had intended to go directly home she now decided to take the path along the bluff and see for herself that the liberty tree stood safe, defiant of all enemies. Rebby's thoughts were filled with a certain fear that Lucia Horton might contrive some new plan to make away with this emblem of freedom; and she gave an exclamation of satisfaction as she saw the handsome young pine, well braced with rocks and timber supports, standing on the bluff.

"The *Polly* will see it first thing when she comes into harbor," thought Rebby, "and nobody will dare fire on it," and vaguely comforted by this thought she started on toward home.

Mr. Weston and Paul were just landing their load of honey, and Rebecca went down to the shore to tell them of the plan for the honey party, of which they both approved. The tubs and buckets were all carried to the Westons' and safely stored away in the big pantry.

Mrs. Foster and Mrs. Weston were talking over arrangements for the next day. Mrs. Foster had suggested that they should each bake a quantity of "spider-cakes." "They are thin and crispy, and will relish well with the honey," she said, and Mrs. Weston agreed, although both the women realized that by making these cakes they would diminish their household stores of Indian meal almost to the danger point. But the *Polly*, with her cargo of wheat flour, sugar, and other necessities, was long overdue; she must soon come to their relief, they thought hopefully; and if she failed to arrive why then they must do their best.

"The neighbors need something cheerful to think of," declared Mrs. Foster, "and I am sure a taste of honey will cheer us all."

The next day was clear and warm with a pleasant southerly wind. Mr. Weston decided to put up some seats under the tall elms, so that the guests could enjoy the spring air. Paul was quite ready to help him; they brought planks from the lumber yard, and long before the first visitor arrived the low comfortable seats were ready.

Anna and Rebby were busy all the morning making small plates of birch-bark, which they stripped from the big logs. These little plates would each hold a square of "spider-cake" and a helping of honey; and as the guests would bring their own cups, to be filled with clear spring water, and their own spoons, the Westons felt that all was ready.

Rebby and Anna both wore their Sunday best, but their dresses were carefully covered by their long pinafores. For they would serve each guest, and it would not do that any careless movement should send a stream of honey over their best gowns. Luretta and Melvina would also help, and had been warned to bring pinafores to wear.

There was a pleasant air of excitement all through the little settlement as the people, dressed in their simple best, walked along the path leading to the Westons'. The minster and his wife, each holding Melvina by the hand, were among the first comers.

"It was a friendly thought to ask your neighbors to share your good fortune," said Mr. Lyon as he greeted Mrs. Weston.

"To tell the truth, 'twas Anna who first thought of it," she responded, and was well pleased when Mrs. Lyon declared that she was not surprised to hear it, as she considered Anna a very thoughtful and generous child.

Rebecca had forgotten for the time her own sense of unworthiness, and was smiling happily as friend after friend arrived, when suddenly her smile vanished. For coming up the path in a fine dress of pale yellow muslin and wearing a flower-trimmed hat was Lucia Horton. No one but Rebecca, of course, was surprised to see Lucia. It was to be expected that she would be a guest at Rebecca's house. Anna and Luretta did not see Lucia's arrival, but Rebby stood quite still, pale and angry, and watched Lucia smiling and speaking to the neighbors. Then Lucia came straight toward Rebecca, and, making an ugly face at her, exclaimed:

"Who is afraid of you, anyway, Rebecca Flora Weston?"

CHAPTER XV

REBBY AND LUCIA

REBBY was too astonished at Lucia's unexpected appearance to make any response to this rude salutation; and, with another scornful glance, Lucia went on her way to where Mrs. Lyon and Mrs. Weston were talking together, and took a seat beside them, and was cordially welcomed by Rebecca's mother, who, of course, knew nothing of the trouble between the two girls.

"Lucia has forgotten her cup and spoon, Rebby; bring her your lustre mug," called Mrs. Weston.

For a moment Rebby pretended not to hear. She was filling the cups with cool spring water, and not until her mother called the second time did she start toward the house for her cherished lustre mug. She was ready to cry at the thought of Lucia's insulting words, and now she must carry the pretty mug to her, and serve her as though she were a welcome guest.

"I won't let her know that I care; and I must be polite because she is a guest, even if she wasn't invited," thought Rebby, as carrying the lustre mug and a birch-bark plate with a square of honeycomb and a brownish crisp "spider-cake" she went toward Lucia.

Neither of the little girls spoke, and Rebby did not look at her former friend who had led her into such sad mischief. Then suddenly there was a crash, a loud cry from Lucia and from Rebby as the lustre mug fell to the ground, and the contents of the frail plate streamed over the delicate yellow muslin of Lucia's fine dress.

"Oh! She has spoiled my dress! She did it on purpose! She did! She did!" wailed Lucia, while Rebecca stood looking at the pieces of her cherished mug that had been brought from Boston when the Westons moved to Machias.

"She dropped it on purpose," Rebby said, but no one seemed to think of her mug. Mrs. Lyon and Mrs. Weston were both endeavoring to comfort Lucia, and to repair the harm done to the yellow muslin. But the honey and water were not easily removed from the delicate fabric.

"I am going home. It's a cheap, foolish party anyway. Honey and water, and corn-bread!" sobbed Lucia angrily, pulling away from the friendly women, and running down the path.

Mrs. Lyon and Mrs. Weston looked after her in amazed disapproval.

"I begin to think there is something in the rumors that Captain Horton and his wife are not trustworthy," Mrs. Lyon said. "The child is so ill-bred she can be but indulged and spoiled at home," and Mrs. Weston agreed. But neither of them imagined that Lucia's mother and father were disloyal to the American cause, and only waiting a profitable opportunity to betray the little settlement to its enemies.

Lucia's angry words cast but a brief shadow over the gathering, and no one noticed that Rebecca had disappeared. At the moment Lucia started for home Rebby had run toward the house. She hurried up the stairs to the little room under the roof where she and Anna slept, and from the closet she drew out the square wooden box that her father had made for her. Her initials R. F. W. were carved inside a small square on the cover, and it had a lock and key. Rebby was very proud of this box, and in it she kept her most treasured possessions: a handkerchief of fine lawn with a lace edge, a pin made from a silver sixpence, and the prayer-book her Grandmother Weston had given her. When Lucia gave her the silk mitts for a birthday present Rebby had put them carefully away with these other treasures. Now she pulled them out hurriedly, and, without waiting to close the box, she ran down the stairs through the kitchen, keeping carefully out of sight of the group under the elm trees, until she could not be seen from the house. Then she caught a glimpse of Lucia's yellow dress, and ran faster than before. But she did not call Lucia's name. She said to herself that she would never speak to Lucia again.

Hearing the hurrying steps behind her Lucia looked over her shoulder, and seeing Rebby she became frightened and ran faster than ever. Lucia did not know why she was afraid, but she remembered that she had not been asked to the party, that she had spoken insultingly to Rebby, and—she had dropped the mug purposely. So it was small wonder that her guilty conscience accused her, and that she was eager to reach home before Rebby could overtake her.

On raced the two girls along the narrow path. A few men at the wharves watched the flying figures, but no one imagined it more than a game. Very soon the Horton house was in sight. Its front door opening on the street stood open to admit the pleasant spring air. In a moment Lucia was in the house and had slammed and fastened the door behind her.

Rebby stood on the step breathless, the silk mitts clasped in her hand. After a moment she rapped loudly on the door. There was no response. But in a moment an upper window opened, and Mrs. Horton looked down at Rebby.

"Why, Rebecca Flora!" she exclaimed in her pleasant voice. "Lucia has gone to your party."

"If you please, Mrs. Horton, I have brought back the mitts Lucia gave me for a birthday present," responded Rebby, her voice faltering a little.

"Oh! Don't they fit? Why, that is a shame. Well, lay them on the step," said Mrs. Horton, wondering why Rebby should look so flushed and warm, and why she had not given the mitts to Lucia. Later on, when she heard Lucia's account of Rebby's turning honey and water over the pretty yellow muslin, she decided that Rebecca was ashamed to keep a gift after treating Lucia so badly.

Rebby went slowly toward home tired and unhappy. All the pleasure of the party, she said to herself, was spoiled. She was not sorry to give up the mitts, for everything that reminded her of Lucia made her think of the night when they had pushed the liberty tree from its moorings.

When she was nearly home she heard Mr. Foster's whistle and in a moment they were face to face.

"Well, Rebecca Flora, 'twas a fine party," he said smilingly, for Mr. Foster had not seen the accident to the mug. "The neighbors are all smiling and cheerful, and we are all the better for meeting in this neighborly fashion," and Mr. Foster ended his sentence with a whistle like a bird's note. "You must come with the others to the liberty pole on Sabbath morning," he added. "Parson Lyon is to preach to us there, and 'twill be a great occasion."

"Yes, sir," Rebby responded, and went slowly on up the slope. It began to seem to her that she would never escape from the liberty pole. And now she met Mr. and Mrs. Lyon, with Melvina dancing along in front of them. "More like Danna than Danna is like herself," thought Rebby, smiling, as she remembered how sedately and quietly Melvina had walked before Danna and Luretta had played their mischievous pranks on the day of the tempest.

The neighbors had all gone when Rebecca reached home, and Mrs. Weston and Anna were in the house, while Mr. Weston and Paul were taking up the seats under the elm trees. The pieces of the broken lustre mug lay on the kitchen table, and Rebby's face clouded as she stood looking at them.

"Lucia Horton dropped it on purpose!" she said. "I know she did."

"And nobody asked her to come to our party," added Anna; " 'twas rude of her to come."

Mrs. Weston looked in astonishment at her two little daughters.

"Not ask Lucia?" she questioned, and listened to Rebby's explanation: that, because of the Hortons' store of dainties, and their scorn of the simple fare of their neighbors, Rebby had decided not to ask Lucia to her party.

But when the little girl had finished her story, Mrs. Weston shook her head disapprovingly.

"I am not pleased with you, Rebecca," she said. " 'Twas not a kind thought to sit in judgment and decide to punish a friend for something that is no fault of hers. Lucia did right to come. Of course she thought you would welcome her."

"She didn't! She didn't!" exclaimed Rebby. "She made up faces at me, and said——"

"Never mind, Rebecca. You see what comes from quarreling. Your mug is broken, Lucia's dress is spoiled, and you had no pleasure from the afternoon. Now, there is something for you to do to put this straight. You must take off your pinafore, put on your sunbonnet, and go straight to Mrs. Horton's and ask Lucia's pardon."

"Oh, Mother!" wailed Rebby. "It isn't fair. It isn't my fault."

But Mrs. Weston was firm. From Rebby's own story her mother decided that she had been unfair to Lucia; she did not ask if Rebby had purposely spilled the honey on Lucia's muslin dress, but she felt it was not the time to allow any ill feeling among the families of the settlement, and that Rebecca's failure to ask the Hortons to come with the other neighbors to taste the wild honey could easily offend them.

Anna stood looking first at Rebby and then at her mother. It was so seldom that Rebby cried, that it seemed a very dreadful thing to her younger sister.

"I'll go, Mother, let me go!" she asked eagerly.

"Do not be so foolish, Anna," responded Mrs. Weston. "This is your sister's duty. It has nothing to do with you. Take off your pinafore, Rebecca, and do as I bid you."

Rebecca was sobbing bitterly. She could not believe that her mother really meant that she should go and ask Lucia Horton's forgiveness.

"If you knew——" she began, tempted to tell her mother all that Lucia had said about the liberty pole, and even what they had done to prevent its erection. But the memory of her promise held her. She knew that her mother expected obedience, and she took off her pinafore, took her sunbonnet, and, still sobbing, went slowly from the room. Anna started to follow her, but Mrs. Weston called her back sharply.

"Anna, you are not to go with your sister," she said, and the little girl came slowly back.

"Oh, dear," she sighed, "I wish Lucia Horton would go sailing off to far lands. To—to Egypt," she concluded. For Anna had never heard much that was pleasant about Egypt, and was sure that all this trouble was Lucia's fault.

Rebecca had never been so unhappy in her life as when she realized that her mother expected her to go to the Hortons' and ask Lucia's pardon for not inviting Mrs. Horton and Lucia to the honey party. There were robins singing in the trees, bluebirds flitting about with gay little notes, and the spring day was full of beauty, but Rebby was not conscious of it as she went slowly along the path.

Very soon she was again standing in front of the Hortons' door, and summoning all her courage she rapped loudly. There was no response, and after a few moments she rapped again; but the house seemed silent and deserted, and no one came to open the door.

And now Rebecca did not know what to do. If she went home she knew that her mother would say that she must return at a later hour to fulfil her errand. So the little girl decided to sit down on the steps and wait for a time.

Twilight was near at hand. The sun was low in the western sky, and a cool little breeze crept up from the river and stirred the tree-tops. Shadows gathered about the house, and still there was no sign or sound of the Hortons, and Rebby was about to start for home when a man came around the corner of the house and spoke to her.

He was evidently a sailor, and in a great hurry. He asked no questions but began speaking as if he had no time to lose.

"Tell your mother that the *Polly* and *Unity* will come into harbor to-morrow, and that Captain Jones is on board the *Unity*. There's a British gunboat

A MAN CAME AROUND THE CORNER OF THE HOUSE

along with them, and your father says there may be trouble, and for you and your mother to keep close indoors until he comes."

The sailor started to move off, but Rebby found courage to ask:

"Where—where are the sloops now?"

"Anchored below Round Island; but we'll be sailing in with morning tide. The Captain bade me keep well out of sight and come straight back to the sloop. Bc sure you tell your mother," responded the man, speaking in such low tones that Rebby had to listen sharply to understand.

"Yes, I'll tell my mother," she replied, and without a moment's hesitation she started for home as fast as her feet could carry her. She had entirely forgotten her anger toward Lucia, or her mother's reproof. All she could think of was the news this sailor, evidently a member of the *Polly*'s crew, had told her, believing that he was speaking to Lucia Horton.

And now Rebecca recalled all that Lucia had told her of what might befall the little village if a British gunboat sailed into harbor and saw a liberty tree flaunting its courageous defiance to injustice. But now she could tell her father, not Lucia's secret, but what the sailor had told her.

"And Father will know what to do. Father and Mr. Lyon," she thought breathlessly, as she ran swiftly up the path and burst into the kitchen, where her father and mother and Anna were waiting her return.

She told her story quickly, and without any mention of what Lucia had confided in her weeks before. "The sailor thought I was Captain Horton's little girl," she concluded.

Mr. Weston questioned Rebby carefully, and then said:

"I'll take this news to Captain O'Brien and to Parson Lyon; but say nothing about it to anyone until we see what news the *Polly* brings." And he hurried away to prepare his neighbors for possible danger.

"You see, Rebby, your obedience may have saved the settlement," said Mrs. Weston, putting her arm about Rebecca.

"But I had not seen Lucia, Mother. I was waiting for her," said Rebecca.

Mrs. Weston made no answer; her thoughts were too full of the possible dangers to the settlement from the British gunboat to think much of the postponed apology; nor was the matter ever again mentioned.

"Now, Rebby, you really have done something for America," declared Anna, as the sisters went up to their room that night. But Rebby shook her head.

"No, Danna, I haven't. But perhaps I can sometime, and you too," she replied. For some reason, that Rebby could not explain even to herself, her thoughts centered around what her father had said on their trip to the Falls of the store of powder and shot at Chandler's River settlement. She had heard her father say that Machias was but ill provided with munitions; and with a British gunboat coming into harbor the next day who could tell how quickly powder and shot might be needed?

CHAPTER XVI

REBBY DECIDES

THE next morning dawned bright and tranquil. The fragrance of pine woods and broad meadows filled the air, and practically all the inhabitants of Machias gathered about the wharves to watch for the *Polly* and *Unity* to come sailing into harbor.

The provisions the sloops were bringing were greatly needed; but when Mr. Weston had told the men of the settlement that the sloops were being convoyed by a British war vessel their alarm and consternation can be imagined. Mrs. Horton and Lucia were about the only ones absent from the wharf when, silently and without a cheer of welcome, the *Polly* and *Unity*, and the boat flying the hated English flag came to anchor.

Captain Jones came ashore, greeting his old-time friends cordially, and explaining that the presence of the gunboat was only to protect him from attacks by British cruisers. But his explanation was received in silence. The memory of the recent battle in Lexington was fresh in the people's hearts, and much as they needed the provisions on the sloops they were ready to do without them unless Captains Horton and Jones could assure their fellow-townsmen of their loyalty and send the British gunboat from the harbor.

Finally he received consent to land his goods, and commenced trading with the people as usual, while the *Margaretta*, the British gunboat, lay at anchor off White's Point, some distance below the town.

Mrs. Lyon received many packages from her Boston relatives, and there were two dolls for Melvina, the ones of which Luretta had spoken on the day when she and Anna had led Melvina to the shore to show her a "clam's nest."

Rebecca's gold beads, intended for her birthday, were safely delivered; and beside the beads was a pair of silk mitts for both Rebby and Anna. To Rebby this seemed a very wonderful thing, and she felt it almost a reward for carrying back those Lucia had given her.

Mrs. Horton now kept Lucia closely at home. Anna and Luretta were invited to spend an afternoon with Melvina, and become acquainted with the new dolls, and Melvina urged Luretta to bring Trit, resolving to dress up the rabbit as she and Anna had done before.

Rebecca was more aware of the troubled condition of the settlement than were these younger girls. Paul Foster told her that his Uncle Benjamin, a bold and energetic man who had served in the old French War, said that the Machias men ought to capture the

British gunboat, and take the sloops, making their captains and crews prisoners. Rebby listened eagerly.

"But we couldn't capture them, Paul; I heard Father say there was but little powder and shot in the settlement," she said.

"We'd get 'em," declared Paul. "If Jones and Horton think they are going to load up their sloops with lumber for British barracks in Boston they'll see trouble."

"And Parson Lyon is not to preach at the liberty pole," said Rebby a little thoughtfully.

Paul made no response to this. He had come up to the Westons' on an errand for his mother, and was now eager to get back to the wharves where the sloops were being unloaded.

"If the Britisher fires on our liberty pole they'll hear a sermon all right," he called back as he ran down the path.

It was difficult for Rebby to attend to the simple duties that her mother required of her. Whenever her father entered the house she watched his face anxiously, half-expecting him to say that the Machias men were ready to capture the gunboat before it could attack the town. When Anna came home eager to describe Melvina's new dolls, and to tell of dressing up Trit, and that London Atus, coming into the room where the little girls were playing and seeing the rabbit wearing a white skirt and bonnet, had turned and run out muttering something about "witches," Rebby listened, but with little interest.

"Danna," she said, as soon as the sisters were alone, "do you suppose you and I could find the way to Chandler's River?"

"Of course we could," Anna declared. "Don't you remember that Father showed us where the trail began, marked by 'spotted' trees?"

"Yes, I remember. Listen, Anna; there is hardly any powder or shot in Machias; if there were the men could protect the liberty pole."

"Yes, yes," Anna responded quickly. "I heard Parson Lyon telling Captain O'Brien that all the men ought to be ready to defend the settlement."

"Oh, Anna! There are quantities of powder stored at Chandler's Mills. Why couldn't we go after it?" Rebby whispered. "Then indeed we would be helping, and perhaps 'twould save the liberty pole."

"Would Father let us?" Anna asked doubtfully.

"Don't you see? We must go after it without telling anyone; then when we bring it back the men can drive off or capture the gunboat," Rebecca explained.

"I think Father ought to know," persisted Anna, so that at last Rebby said no more, after Anna had promised not to repeat Rebby's plan to anyone.

But Rebby slept but little that night. If the gunboat fired on the town she felt it would be her fault for having kept Lucia's secret to herself; and yet she dared not break a promise. In some way Rebby felt that she must do something to make right her foolish act in helping Lucia set the liberty tree adrift.

The next day Captain Jones began his preparations to load the sloops with lumber for Boston, and the Machias men, doubtful of the Captain's loyalty, determined that the sloops should not return to Boston. Rebby and Anna were in the lumber yard filling a basket with chips, when a number of men talking of this decision passed them.

"If we only had more powder and shot," said one; "but we cannot spare a single man to go to Chandler's River after supplies."

"There, Anna!" exclaimed Rebby. "Did you hear what those men said? Do you not see that we can help as much as a real soldier? We can go to Chandler's River. We must."

"Perhaps Father would give us permission if we asked him," Anna persisted. But Rebecca shook her head at this suggestion; she dared not risk the chance of a refusal.

"We ought to go at once," she said earnestly. "'Twill be a long tramp, and the gunboat may come up the harbor and threaten the settlement any day. Do say you will go, Anna."

Rebby knew that Anna's knowledge of the forest, her strength and courage, would be all that could enable her to undertake the task. Without Anna she feared that she might fail in finding her way, and never reach Chandler's River.

"Think, Danna! The gunboat will shoot down our liberty pole! Perhaps burn the church and our houses, and they may carry off our father a prisoner! 'Tis what they try to do whenever Americans resist; and if the Machias men have powder and shot they'll not let the gunboat come near. And we can get the powder and save the settlement. Oh, Danna——"

Rebby's petition ended in a wail.

And now Anna was as eager to start as Rebby herself. The thought of her father being taken a prisoner and that she and Rebby could prevent so great a misfortune made her no longer hesitate.

"We will start to-morrow morning, early," she said. "We must make sure that our moccasins are in good shape, Rebby; and we must take some cornbread, for 'twill be a good journey. How early can we start, Rebby?"

"Before sunrise, surely," responded Rebby, "and I will write on a strip of birch-bark what we are going to do, and pin it to Father's hat. Then they will not worry about us."

"Worry! Why, Father will think it a brave deed," declared Anna. "I wish we had started this morning."

That day seemed very long to the sisters. They made their preparations carefully for the next day's journey, and at an early hour went to bed, so that they might awaken in good season.

The next morning dawned clear. Before the sun was up Anna was wide awake, and at her whispered "Rebby," her sister's eyes opened quickly, and they slipped quietly out of bed. In a few moments they were fully dressed for their tramp through the forest. Very cautiously they made their way down the stairs. The house was silent. Neither Mr. nor Mrs. Weston heard the faintest sound to disturb their slumbers.

On the piece of smooth birch-bark that Rebby had made ready on the previous day, with a bit of charcoal from the fireplace she wrote:

"Dear Mother and dear Father: Anna and I arc going to Chandler's River to bring home powder and shot for Machias men to use to save the settlement. We will be home to-morrow. Your loving Rebby and Danna."

They slipped this under the deerskin thong that was twisted about Mr. Weston's hat, opened the kitchen door gently, and moved noiselessly along in the shadow of the house, then ran swiftly up the path, and in a short time were out of sight of the houses of the settlement.

"Now we must walk slowly for a time," cautioned Anna, remembering her father's warnings against hurrying at the beginning of a tramp. "We must go on steadily for a time, and rest before we begin to feel tired. That is the way Indians do, and Father says it is why they can travel day after day and not be exhausted."

Rebby looked at her little sister admiringly. In woodland lore she realized that Danna was much wiser than herself, and she was quite ready to be guided by her.

When Mrs. Weston called the girls the next morning and received no response she was not greatly surprised, as they often slept a little later than their parents. "The extra sleep will do them no harm," she said smilingly, as she and Mr. Weston sat down to the breakfast table; therefore Rebby and Danna were well on their way before their father took his hat from its accustomed place and discovered the strip of birch-bark with its surprising message.

Mr. Weston read the note, and stood for a moment silent, thinking what could be done. His first impulse was to hasten after his girls and bring them safely home. Then came the thought of the peril of the settlement. At any moment he might be called upon to help in its defense. Every man would be needed. He recalled Danna's strength and fearlessness, and her knowledge of the forest, and Rebby's quiet good judgment. If there were dangers he believed his girls could meet them fearlessly. Then, too, what a blessing it would be to have them bring home a store of powder and shot. It would mean the salvation of the settlement. Mr. Weston began to feel very proud of his little daughters and to feel sure they would return safely.

"What is the trouble with your hat, Father?" questioned his wife. "You stand looking at it as if it had some message for you."

"Indeed it has," Mr. Weston replied smilingly. "It tells me that we have two of the bravest girls in America. Listen," and he read Rebby's note aloud.

"'Tis a deed to make us proud," he said, "and 'twill give new courage to every man in the settlement to know that a supply of powder will be here to-morrow."

But it was a long and anxious day for Mrs. Weston. She knew the perils of the forest, and her thoughts centered about lurking bears that might spring out upon Rebby and Danna as they went through the wilderness. She endeavored to find comfort by remembering that their errand was for the cause of justice and freedom, and that a love stronger than her own was about them.

CHAPTER XVII

A PERILOUS JOURNEY

NOT until the girls reached the beginning of the forest trail, where their father had pointed out the dim path leading toward Chandler's River, did they feel really sure that their father would not follow them. But as they stopped for a brief rest under the shadow of a wide-spreading beech tree Rebby said:

"Father could have overtaken us by this time, Danna, if he did not think it was right for us to go."

Danna agreed cheerfully, and now both the girls felt a new courage for this perilous undertaking that was sure to tax their strength to the utmost. The fact that their father had not hastened after them made them both realize how important it was that powder and shot should reach the Machias settlement as soon as possible.

The faint path soon disappeared entirely, and had Rebby been alone she would not have known which way to turn. But Anna went on confidently, keeping a sharp outlook for the "blazed" trees of which her father had told her as marking the way toward Chandler's River.

They forced their way through dense masses of tangled underbrush, over fallen trees, and through the shadowy stretches of thickly growing pine. Now and then they came to some marshy stretch, which Anna would carefully avoid, for she remembered how often her father had warned her of the dangers of such places, with their unmarked quicksands that would quickly swallow the heedless person who ventured upon them.

Notwithstanding Anna's caution in regard to resting frequently they pushed on steadily, with but one stop until the sound of water as it dashed over a rocky bed warned them that they were near Whitneyville Falls, and half-way to their destination.

The sun was now directly overhead, and as they came out from the shade of the forest to the open space along the river's bank Rebby sank down on the grass with a long breath of relief.

"I never was so tired in all my life," she declared.

"We will take a good rest and eat our corn-bread," responded Anna. "I am sure the remainder of the way will not be so hard, because we can follow the river up to the settlement."

Rebby was too tired to reply. She stretched herself out on the wand grass and closed her eyes.

"Poor Rebby," thought Danna, looking down at her elder sister and remembering that Rebecca had never enjoyed woodland tramps, and realizing that this undertaking was much harder for her sister than for herself.

"She's asleep," Anna whispered to herself, with a little smile of satisfaction. "Now I will have a fine surprise for her when she awakes," and the little girl tiptoed noiselessly back to the edge of the woods, where she had noticed a quantity of checkerberry leaves. There were many crimson berries still clinging to the vines, and Anna picked these carefully, using her cap for a basket, and gathering a quantity of the young checkerberry leaves. "Rebby is sure to like these," she thought happily.

Anna's sharp glance moved about quickly and finally rested near an old stump.

"Partridge eggs!" she exclaimed joyfully, and in a moment she was beside the stump peering down at a circle of small brownish eggs. She counted them, and before she had whispered "twenty!" a whining, scrambling noise close at hand told her that the partridge to whom the eggs belonged was close at hand.

"You won't miss a few eggs, Mistress Partridge," said Anna soberly, carefully selecting four from the outer edge of the circle, and then going softly away, that she might not unnecessarily frighten the woodland bird.

She now carried the cap with great care, as she looked about hoping to discover some sign of a woodland spring. She kept along at the edge of the woods, and very soon she heard the sound of a noisy little brook hurrying along to the river. It was not far up the river from the place where Rebby was so comfortably asleep, and Anna decided that it would be just the place for their noonday luncheon.

She set the cap, with all its treasures, carefully under the shade of a tiny fir tree near the side of the brook and then ran back to awaken Rebby.

"Dinner is ready!" she called gaily as she ran; and the sound of her voice made Rebecca sit up quickly, and exclaim:

"The British will shoot down our liberty pole!" For her dreams had been of soldiers in red coats firing at the liberty pole, while Mr. Worden Foster, with a big pitchfork, tried to drive them away.

"It is a truly dinner, with eggs," declared Anna happily, as she led the way back to the noisy little brook.

The raw eggs tasted good to the hungry girls, and the good corn-bread and spicy berries and tender checkerberry leaves, with cool water to drink, made them both feel refreshed and rested, and ready for the remaining distance to Chandler's River settlement.

They crossed the little brook and went sturdily on. Now and then a partridge flew in front of them. Squirrels scolded and chattered among the tree tops, and once or twice a rabbit leaped out from behind some stump and ran ahead of them as if daring them to capture him.

Both the girls well knew that there were larger and more dangerous animals in the forests. There were bears prowling somewhere in those dim shadowy woods, eating the young buds and leaves, and capturing such defenseless birds and rabbits as they could. Once or twice they heard some heavy creature crashing through the underbrush, and looked at each other with startled eyes; but no harm came near them, and by the middle of the afternoon they reached the first house of the settlement, and had told their errand.

"Every man in the settlement is on his way to Machias this very hour," declared the friendly woman who had welcomed the girls with amazed admiration; and, when they told of the scarcity of powder and shot in Machias, had said that the men of Chandler's River settlement had believed Machias well supplied with powder, and had taken but a small quantity with them.

"One of our fishermen brought news of the British gunboat, and our men started at once. They went by the lower trail," explained the woman, as she stirred the hot porridge she was cooking for the girls' supper.

"'Tis well your parents had courage to let you come, and you must rest, and get early to bed. I will go to the powder-house and bring back as much as you can carry, and I will go with you a part of the way to-morrow," she added, and Rebecca and Danna thanked her gratefully. After they had eaten their porridge they were quite ready to bathe their tired feet in the hot water their hostess had ready, and go to bed, although the sun was yet an hour above the horizon.

While the girls slept Mrs. Getchell hurried to the other houses of the settlement, telling the story of the two courageous girls who had come through the forest on their patriotic errand.

" 'Tis hardly to be believed," she declared. "These little maids are brave as soldiers, and they will carry the powder and shot back in good time to be of use. General Washington shall hear of them, and the Province of Maine will not forget their names."

The women and children listened eagerly, and all were anxious for a sight of the little maids who had shown such courage and hardihood. But Mrs. Getchell declared that they must not be disturbed, or they would not be equal to the return journey on the next day.

"But you can all come in the morning and see them start for Machias," she said, and with the powder and shot, ten pounds of each, safely packed, she returned home.

It was broad daylight when Rebecca and Anna awoke. Mrs. Getchell had breakfast ready for them, and they enjoyed the hot batter cakes and maple syrup and the rich milk. They had not finished eating when a murmur of voices outside the door made them look up in surprise.

"'Tis the women and children," explained Mrs. Getchell smilingly. "They have come to wish you good fortune."

Rebecca and Anna hardly knew what to say as the women of the settlement entered the big kitchen, and with friendly smiles praised the two girls for their courage and loyalty. Boys and girls of their own age gathered about the doorway and looked at them admiringly; and when Mrs. Getchell said it was time to start, and with Rebby and Anna led the way toward the river, young and old followed them. One of the older women slipped a slender gold chain around Anna's neck, saying: "Wear it, dear little maid, to remind you that there is no sacrifice too great to make for America's freedom." And a little girl of about Rebecca's age shyly pressed a little purse into her hand. "'Tis a golden sovereign that my mother bade me give you," she said, "and my mother says that always the children of Maine will remember what you have done for America's cause."

Rebby hardly knew what to reply. "If they knew that I set the liberty tree afloat they would not praise me," she thought unhappily.

A short distance beyond the settlement the women and children bade the girls good-bye, with many good wishes for their safe return to Machias. But Mrs. Getchell was to go on with them for a part of their journey.

As Rebby and Anna turned to wave their hands to these new friends a loud cheer went up, the boys waving their caps and the girls calling: "Good luck to the brave little maids from Machias."

Mrs. Getchell went on with them for several miles, carrying the powder and shot, and a flat package containing food for their journey. She told them to follow the river down, as that trail was more traveled and over smoother ground, although farther to travel than the forest trail; and kissing the girls good-bye, after they had promised to visit her "as soon as the English had been sent home," she turned back toward the settlement.

Rebby and Danna watched Mrs. Getchell's stout figure until it was hidden by the forest, and then, more serious and anxious than at any time during their perilous undertaking, they picked up the heavy packages that Mrs. Getchell had placed on the trunk of a fallen tree, and prepared to continue their journey.

The shot was in two strong bags, while the powder, in order that it might be kept perfectly dry and safe, was in two tin canisters, each one carefully sewn up in stout sailcloth. Mrs. Getchell had fastened a stout strap to each bag of powder and a bag of shot. These straps went over the girls' shoulders, and made them easier to carry than in any other way. It was of course a tough job for each girl to carry ten pounds for the long distance that lay before them, but they pushed on valiantly.

At first the river trail was fairly smooth, and they made good progress, but after a few miles they encountered a long stretch of rocky ground. Here they had to clamber over high ledges, or else go a long distance out of their way. Before noonday Rebby declared that she could not go another step, and sat down at the foot of a high mass of rocks over which they must climb.

"You will have to go on and leave me, Danna," she said. "My feet won't go, they are so tired; and my shoulders ache."

The day had grown very warm; there was not a breath of air, and Anna owned that she had never seen so difficult a trail. Mrs. Getchell had warned them to be sure and keep in sight of the river and it would lead them straight to Machias. As Anna looked at her sister she began to fear that they might not be able to reach home before night, and she knew all the danger and peril that a night spent in that lonely spot would mean.

They had not found a spring or brook since leaving Mrs. Getchell, and they were both very thirsty as well as tired and hungry.

"We will take a good rest, Rebby, and eat our luncheon. I saw Mrs. Getchell stirring up a molasses cake while we ate breakfast," said Anna, encouragingly, "and she put a tin dipper with the luncheon. See!" and Anna held up the small cup-shaped dish. "I'll fetch you a drink from the river," she added, and putting her burden of powder and shot on the ground beside Rebby, she made her way down the steep bank of the river.

The bank was covered by a thick growth of alders, with here and there a small spruce tree. Anna wondered how she would ever manage to bring a cup filled with water up that bank; but she kept on, and was soon at the river's edge. The rushing water was clear and cool, and Anna drank thirstily. Then she bathed her face and hands, slipped off her moccasins and stockings and dipped her feet in the cool stream. She felt rested and refreshed, as with the tin cup filled with water, and covered with a broad leaf of a water-lily, she made her careful way back to where she had left her sister.

Rebby had taken off her hat and moccasins. She drank the water eagerly before saying a word.

"I feel better already," she said, "and by the time we have eaten our lunch I know we can start. We *must,*" she added soberly, "for if we do not get home before dark Father will surely start after us."

Danna was opening the package of food and made no response, but she was wondering if Rebby could really hold out until they reached the settlement. "I couldn't leave her alone," the little girl thought a little fearfully, wondering if their long journey was, after all, to end in failure. For she knew that if they did not reach Machias by the early evening their attempt to aid the settlement would have been in vain.

"Look, Rebby! White bread, spread with butter," she said, as she unfastened the package, "and here are slices of chicken, and big squares of molasses cake," and Rebby smiled at her little sister's evident delight. The two girls thoroughly enjoyed the excellent food, and when the last crumb had been eaten Rebecca declared herself rested, and ready to start on.

As she picked up her moccasins she exclaimed: "Oh, Danna!" in so tragic a tone that her sister looked at her with frightened eyes.

"What is it, Rebby?" she whispered.

"A hole in my moccasin. Look!" and Rebby held up the moccasin, showing a long narrow slit on the sole. "These awful rocks! I can never walk without cutting my foot, and then I can't walk at all."

"I can fix it," Danna declared instantly. "Give it to me, Rebby; quick!" and the elder sister obeyed.

Danna reached into the pocket of her doeskin skirt and drew out her sharp clasp-knife; very carefully she cut a broad strip from the top of Rebby's moccasin, and skilfully fitted it inside over the sole.

"I saw Father do this very thing once," she said. "It will surely last until we reach home."

"I knew I could never make this trip without you, Danna," Rebby said gratefully. "You are as wise as a real little Indian girl."

They went on now at a slower pace, for both girls realized that if Rebby was again overcome by heat and fatigue that it might be impossible for her to continue. Even Danna owned to herself that she had never been so tired. The strap across her shoulders, supporting the heavy load, pressed heavily and at times became almost unbearable; but not for a moment did it occur to Danna to relinquish the burden.

They had left the rocky stretch behind them and come out to a comparatively smooth pasture. The deep forest lay on their right; to the left was the sloping bank leading to the river. Suddenly Anna stopped short and grasped Rebby's arm; a second later a deer leaped directly across their path and plunged down the bank, followed by a leaping, panting creature that hardly seemed to touch the ground.

"A bear!" whispered Rebby with frightened eyes.

"Hurry, Rebby," responded Danna, and the girls, forgetting their tired feet and lame shoulders, sped silently over the open pasture land.

Danna was the first to speak, but it was in a whisper: "We need not fear, Rebby. He was after the deer."

Rebby made no response. More fully than ever the elder girl realized the peril into which she had led her younger sister. But nevertheless she whispered to herself that it was the only way: the powder and shot were all that could save the settlement from the hands of the enemy.

The girls did not stop again to rest, nor did they speak until they reached the top of a rise of ground from which they could see the first houses of the settlement. The sun was dropping behind the tall pines on the western side of the river, and they could see the *Polly* and *Unity* as they lay at anchor in the harbor.

"We are safe now, Danna," said Rebby thankfully, and the sisters smiled at each other happily.

"Can't we leave the powder and shot here?" pleaded Danna, twisting the uncomfortable strap into an easier position. "Father would come and get it, and it's so heavy."

But Rebby shook her head. "It would not be safe. We must carry it straight home," she said; so, with a sigh of endurance, Danna started on.

They were now in the broad trail that led straight to the little settlement, and before they reached the first house they saw a tall figure striding toward them. It was Mr. Weston, and in a moment their load of powder and shot was swung over his shoulders, Rebby was clasping one hand and Anna the other, and they were both talking at once, trying to tell him the story of their journey.

Their mother came running down the path to meet them, and clasped them in her thankful embrace. The Westons had not told their neighbors of the girls' undertaking, thinking it wiser to await their return; but as soon as Rebby and Anna were safely indoors their father hastened away to tell the men of the settlement that a supply of powder and shot had been brought to Machias by his courageous daughters.

CHAPTER XVIII

TRIUMPH

THE day following the return of Rebecca and Anna Weston from their perilous and difficult undertaking to bring the much needed powder and shot to Machias was Sunday, the eleventh of June, 1775.

Very early that morning there was an air of unusual excitement about the little settlement. It was known that the English officers from the gunboat would attend service in the meeting-house that morning; and the Machias men had decided, with the approval of Parson Lyon, to surround the church and capture them before they had time to carry out their plans against the settlement.

Rebby and Danna were eating their breakfast when Captain Benjamin Foster appeared at the kitchen door, saying that he had come to thank them for their courageous effort to aid the men in defending their rights. As he entered the room the girls jumped up from their seats at the table and curtseyed; and as he went on to praise their loyalty and valor, the two little girls, hand in hand, stood before him with downcast eyes, flushed and happy at his approving words.

In spite of anxious thoughts as to the result of the conflict between the men of Machias and the English soldiers, Mrs. Weston was very proud and happy that morning as she walked to church with Rebecca and Anna beside her. Many neighbors stopped them to praise the little girls, and all declared that the people of the settlement would always remember what they had done.

Even Parson Lyon and his wife were waiting at the church door to speak to the two little heroines; and Melvina and Luretta felt as if they shared in their friends' honors as they walked up the aisle of the church beside them.

Before the English officers had landed from their boat a number of the Machias men had quietly hidden their guns in the building; while Captain Benjamin Foster, with men armed and ready for action, were concealed among the tall pines close at hand, ready to surround the church and seize the English officers; and had they taken London Atus into their confidence this well-prepared scheme might have succeeded.

But London was entirely innocent of any trouble near at hand. From his place in a side pew he kept a watchful eye upon Melvina, and perhaps wondered a little at all the attention lavished on the little Weston girls.

Rebby saw Captain and Mrs. Horton and Lucia, with Captain Jones, enter the church. Lucia did not look toward the group of girls seated in the Westons' pew. The Hortons were no longer trusted by their neighbors, and after that morning in church they vanished from the community and never returned.

Rebby's glance now rested on London. How queerly he looked, she thought wonderingly. He was leaning sideways peering out of an open window. As Rebecca watched him he rose to his feet with a loud cry, and before any restraining word could reach him he had leaped through the open window.

In a moment all was confusion. There were loud cries of "Stop him!" Men rushed from the church, but the English officers, followed by Captain Jones and the Hortons, had scrambled through the open windows and were well on their flight toward their boats, which they reached in safety, although numerous shots were fired after them. The gunboat at once turned her guns on the town. Shot after shot echoed across the quiet waters of the harbor, but the range was too long, and no harm was done.

The women and children huddled in the pews of the church, until Parson Lyon, musket in hand, came up from the shore to tell them that all was quiet and to return to their homes.

Melvina and Anna left the church together, and Luretta and Rebby followed with Mrs. Weston. Melvina said good-bye to her friends very soberly, and clasped her father's hand very closely as they walked toward home.

"Will the English soldiers shoot down our liberty pole, Father?" she asked.

"The English captain has sent us word that we are to take it down before sunset, so that he may be saved that trouble," replied Parson Lyon, his tone indicating that he considered the English captain's remark as an amusing utterance, not to be seriously considered.

"But it will not be taken down," said Melvina confidently.

"Indeed it will not. And had that scamp London but held his peace instead of mistaking Captain Foster's men for an armed enemy marching upon us, the English would be our prisoners at this moment," declared her father. "But that is but postponed," he added quietly, "and to-morrow morning Machias men will give the English captain a lesson."

There were many anxious hearts in the settlement that night, for it had been determined that in the early dawn of the following morning the men should seize the sloop *Unity*, and make the attempt to capture the English gunboat. Neither Rebecca nor Anna knew of this plan; and, still tired from their journey, as well as by the excitement that morning at the church, they were glad to go early to bed and were soon sound asleep. Mrs. Weston, unable to sleep, waited in the kitchen for her husband's return. For Mr. Weston and his neighbors were busy with their preparations for the coming battle. It was decided that Captain O'Brien should take command of the sloop, and before the sun rose the next morning forty Machias men were on board the *Unity*. Half this number were armed with broad-axes and pitchforks; the remainder had muskets.

It was just at sunrise when a warning shot from the gunboat reverberated along the harbor, and Rebecca awakened suddenly. She realized at once that the conflict had begun. In an instant she was out of bed, slipped quickly into her clothing, and leaving Danna sound asleep, she sped down the path and along the trail to the high bluff that commanded a view of the harbor.

There was a favoring wind and the *Unity*, with her crew of untrained men, was now in full chase of a vessel well-armed and equipped. On swept the sloop, and a sudden volley of musketry from her deck astonished and confused the enemy. The gunboat swerved, and the bowsprit of the *Unity* plunged into her mainsail, holding the two vessels together for a brief moment.

Rebecca, standing on the bluff, shouted aloud. She was sure that the moment of triumph for the Machias men was close at hand. But victory was not so easily achieved; the vessels suddenly parted, and now a storm of bullets rained upon the *Unity*.

Captain O'Brien swung the sloop alongside the *Margaretta* and twenty of his men armed with pitch-forks sprang to the enemy's deck. A hand-to-hand conflict ensued. Surprised by the dauntless valor of the Machias men the English were forced to yield. The English flag was pulled down amid triumphant shouts of the Americans; the wounded were cared for, and English officers and crew made prisoners of war.

When Rebecca saw the English flag vanish from the gunboat's mast and heard the resounding cheers, she knew that the Americans had conquered their enemy, and that the liberty tree would stand unchallenged. But she did not realize that she had been a witness to the first naval exploit in America after the battle of Lexington.

All the women and children and such men as had been left behind, were now hurrying toward the wharves. Cheer after cheer rang out across the harbor as the *Unity* and the captured gunboat came slowly to their anchorage.

Mrs. Weston and Anna came hurrying down the path and Rebby ran to meet them.

"I saw the battle, Mother!" she exclaimed eagerly. "I was on the bluff and saw it all." But before Mrs. Weston could respond to this astonishing statement a boat-load of men from the *Unity* had landed.

"Your father is safe," whispered Mrs. Weston, "and now let me see of what use I can be to the wounded men. Rebby, take Anna back to the house and stay there until I come."

The two little girls walked silently back to the house. The battle that had been so feared was over; the enemy was conquered, and Rebecca and Anna knew that by their bringing the powder from Chandler's River they had helped to win the conflict. But just then they did not think of that. They could think only of the wounded men, who had been so carefully brought on shore by their companions.

On the following day the inhabitants, such as were not caring for the wounded English and American soldiers, gathered at the liberty pole. It was a quiet and reverent gathering. Several men of the settlement had been wounded, and two had given their lives for America's cause. Parson Lyon gave loving tribute to these heroes, as he offered thanks for the triumph of loyalty.

And then, before all the people, he praised Rebecca and Anna Weston for their courage in undertaking the difficult and dangerous journey through the wilderness to bring aid to the settlement.

"Step forward, Rebecca and Anna Weston," he said smilingly; and, a little fearfully, the sisters, hand in hand, left their mother's side and approached the liberty pole. Taking each by the hand Parson Lyon smiled down upon them.

There was a little murmur of approval among the people, and one by one the older members of the congregation came forward and praised the little girls.

"It is Rebby who should be praised, not me," Anna insisted. "It is not fair for me to be praised." While Rebecca, in her turn, declared eagerly that she could never have brought home the powder without Anna's help.

There were many hard and troublous days ahead for the little settlement, but their courage did not falter. The valor of the Machias men was speedily recognized by the Provincial Congress of Massachusetts, who, on June 26, 1775, passed a resolution extending to them the thanks of the Congress for their courageous conduct. The news of the brilliant victory was heralded throughout the land, stimulating the colonists everywhere to emulate the example of the courageous settlers of Machias.

Rebecca often thought of her former friend, Lucia Horton; but she never told the story of the night when, misled by Lucia's plausible story, she had tried to defeat the loyalty of the settlers by setting their liberty tree adrift. As she looked up at the tall sapling, the emblem of the loyalty of the settlement, she was proud indeed that she had been of use in its protection.

Anna's gold chain was her greatest treasure. It was shown to every little girl in the settlement, and each one knew its story. The golden sovereign given to Rebecca was no less highly prized.

"That sovereign has a value beyond money. It is a medal for valor," her father said; and on the year when peace was firmly established between England and America Rebecca's golden sovereign was smoothed, and upon it these words were engraved:

"Presented
to
A Brave Little
Maid of Maine,
For Loyalty,
June, 1775."

The Stories in This Series Are:

A LITTLE MAID OF PROVINCETOWN
A LITTLE MAID OF MASSACHUSETTS COLONY
A LITTLE MAID OF NARRAGANSETT BAY
A LITTLE MAID OF OLD PHILADELPHIA
A LITTLE MAID OF OLD NEW YORK
A LITTLE MAID OF OLD CONNECTICUT
A LITTLE MAID OF TICONDEROGA
A LITTLE MAID OF VIRGINIA
A LITTLE MAID OF MARYLAND
A LITTLE MAID OF MOHAWK VALLEY
A LITTLE MAID OF OLD MAINE